Stock Market Forecasting

The McWhirter Method

De-Mystified

M.G. Bucholtz, B.Sc., MBA

Disclaimer

A Wood Dragon Book

Box 1216, Regina, Saskatchewan, Canada, S4P 3B4

Copyright 2014 Malcolm Bucholtz

Published by Wood Dragon Books

DEDICATION

For Jeanne

CONTENTS

FIGURES

EXERCISES

INTRODUCTION

I was first introduced to the works of the mysterious Louise McWhirter in 2012 when I attended the United Astrology Conference in New Orleans, USA.

After attending this event, where I had purchased a re-printed version of her epic 1937 book, I read and re-read it nearly twenty times. Her methodology is anything but straightforward.

Straightforward it may not be, but powerful it certainly is. So powerful in fact that in early 2014 I decided to share my understanding of her methodology with the many visitors to my website and with the many subscribers to my Astrology E-Alert newsletter. I created a manuscript entitled *De-Mystifying the McWhirter Theory of Stock Market Forecasting – A Study Guide.* I did not assign an ISBN number to this effort, instead opting to simply sell copies of the self-published product via my website.

The response to this initial creation has been better than expected. In August 2014 I made the decision to assign an ISBN number to this effort and the book you now hold in your hands is the end result. Although it is not called a study guide, I have retained the study guide format throughout. The best way to become well versed in the McWhirter methodology is by way of hands-on learning. This is why throughout this book you will be encouraged to create horoscope charts and you will also be treated to practical exercises.

Once you have worked your way through this book, you will be in possession of a skill set that few other traders and investors have.

Your journey towards a truly unique way of looking at the financial markets begins now.

1. WHO WAS LOUISE MCWHIRTER?

Very little is known about Louise McWhirter, except that in 1937 she wrote the book *McWhirter Theory of Stock Market Forecasting.*

In my travels to places as far away as the British Library in London, England to research the subject of financial astrology, not once did I come across any other books by her. Not once did I find any other book from her era that even mentioned her name. All of this I find to be deeply mysterious.

I am of the opinion that the name Louise McWhirter may have been a *nom de plume,* or as we say in English – *a pen name,* for a writer seeking to conceal his or her identity – and for good reason. In the early decades of the 20th century many American States still had arcane statute laws that could be traced back to the days of the Salem Witch Trials. These statute laws prohibited the commercial use of occult science. That is, you could not openly set up a shop to conduct tarot card readings or perform palm reading analyses. And using astrology to predict the stock market – well, that too would have been illegal.

Despite these laws, the early decades of the 20th century saw many successful traders on Wall Street use astrology as a tool to gauge the markets. The underlying premise of their efforts was that events in our cosmos influence our emotions. These changing emotions then impact our buying and selling decisions which make stock prices, commodity prices and market indices rise and fall. Chief among the many traders who used astrology was the respected W.D. Gann. I suspect that one of these traders, (perhaps even Gann himself) seeking to write a book documenting his astrology methodology for the benefit of future generations, concocted the *pen name* Louise McWhirter as the author for his book. But, no matter who wrote *McWhirter Theory of Stock Market Forecasting*, the methodology outlined in it was accurate in the late 1930s and remains accurate today. The trader or investor having a comfortable grasp on this methodology will enjoy a distinct advantage over those traders and investors who are unwilling to make the connection between human emotion and stock market price movements.

2. THREE COMPONENTS

There are three components to the McWhirter approach.

The first component involves the transit of the North Node around the zodiac wheel. It takes 18.6 years for the Node to complete a full transit. When the Node moves through certain signs, the economic business cycle reaches a low point and when the Node is in certain other signs, the business cycle is at its strongest.

The second component of the McWhirter approach pertains to the New York Stock Exchange which was founded in May 1792. The McWhirter approach focuses on the Moon and its 29 day lunar cycle. There are several key features that one can note in the 1792 horoscope chart for the New York Stock Exchange. By studying the planetary positions in the zodiac wheel at the time of a New Moon, one can identify additional key features. As the 29 day lunar cycle progresses, by watching for times when Moon and other planets make aspects to these various key features, one can identify times when there will be a strong probability of a short term trend change (inflection point) on the New York Stock Exchange.

The third part of the McWhirter approach pertains to individual stocks and commodity futures. By studying the First Trade horoscope chart of a stock or commodity future, one can identify key planets and critical planetary aspects. By watching times when the transiting Sun and various transiting planets make aspects to these key positions, one can identify times during a calendar year when there will be a strong likelihood for a trend change.

The McWhirter approach has many subtleties and nuances. But, with the aid of this book - once you have become comfortable with the McWhirter method, you will be in possession of and talented in a skill that few other traders and investors have.

3. BASIC ASTROLOGY

The *zodiac wheel* is comprised of 12 sections. Each section contains 30 degrees. Twelve sections of 30 degrees each equate to 360 degrees or a full circle. Each section of the zodiac wheel bears a name which is steeped in ancient mythology. Figure 1 presents these names and the symbol that is associated with each name. If you are not already well versed in identifying these var ous symbols on a horoscope wheel, take some time before reading further to get to know them better.

♈	Aries	♎	Libra
♉	Taurus	♏	Scorpio
♊	Gemini	♐	Sagittarius
♋	Cancer	♑	Capricorn
♌	Leo	♒	Aquarius
♍	Virgo	♓	Pisces

Figure 1 The Zodiac Signs

When we hear the word *horoscope*, we immediately think of the astrological predictions that appear in our daily newspapers. But, such verbiage is not what a horoscope really is. When planetary positions are denoted on a zodiac wheel, that wheel is then commonly referred to as a *horoscope*. This word is taken from the Greek *horoskopus* meaning *'a look at the hours'*.

The various planets in a typical horoscope are also illustrated by symbols. Figure 2 presents these symbols. In addition to planetary symbols, there are a couple other features that are also important. In a horoscope chart the notations MC and Asc will appear. The Asc (Ascendant) refers to the astrological sign that was on the eastern horizon at the time the horoscope was created. The MC (Mid Heaven) refers to the astrological sign that was in the south, 90 degrees from the Asc. If you are not already well versed in identifying these various symbols on a horoscope wheel, take some time before reading further to get to know them better.

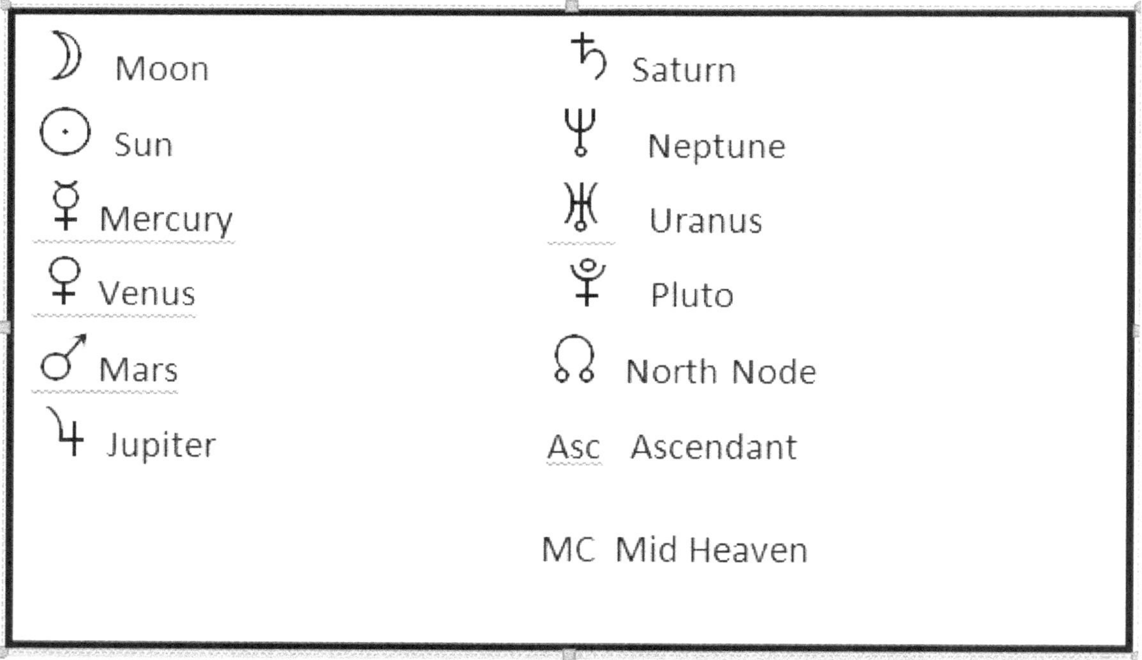

Figure 2 Planetary Signs

The inner portion of a horoscope is divided into 12 sections, numbered 1 through 12 going in a counter-clockwise fashion. These divisions are called *Houses.* The concept of a House is purely a mathematical one. There are many ways of dividing a horoscope into Houses, with each method differing only slightly from the other. This book will use Placidus House divisions. Please note that House divisions are not the same as the twelve astrological sign divisions.

Throughout this publication you will see numerous horoscopes presented and numerous references made to various planets. Whenever uncertain as to a particular sign or symbol, just refer back to this section.

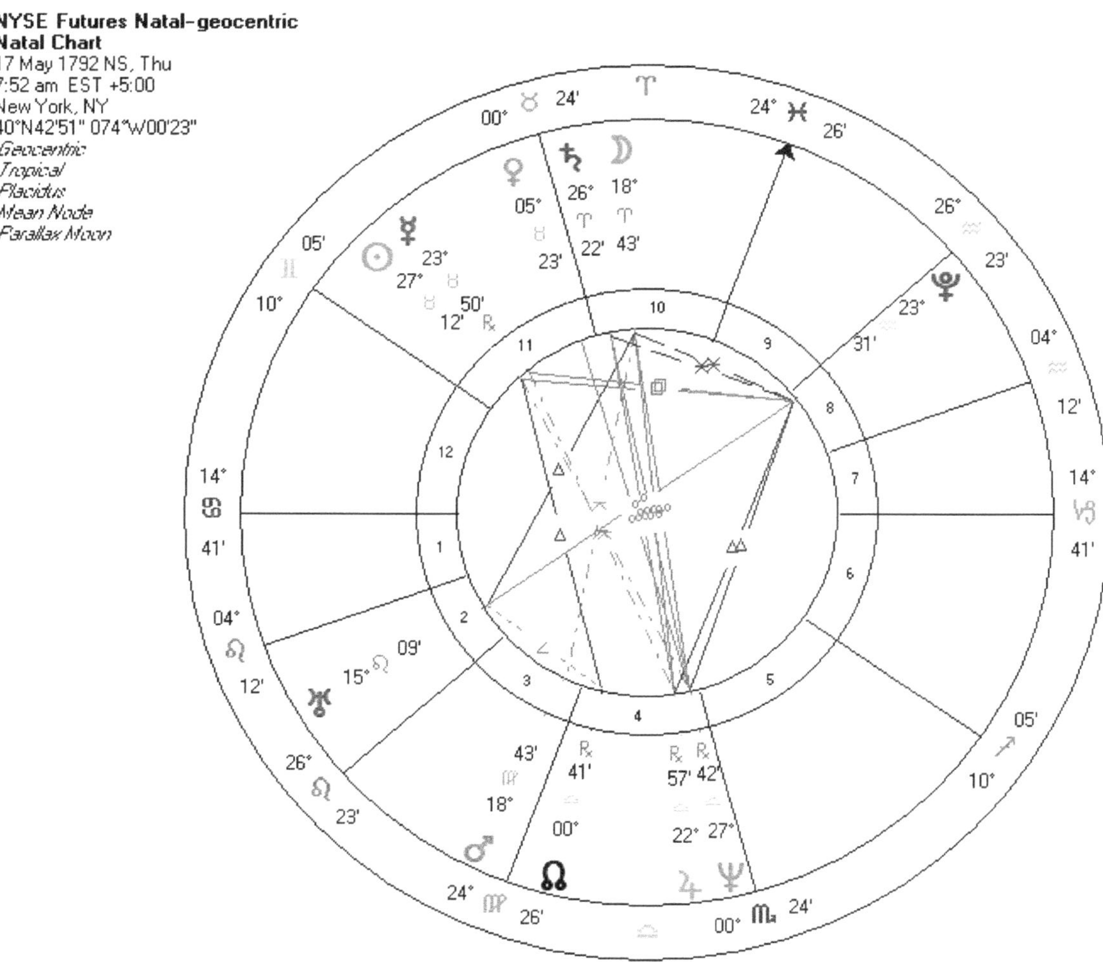

Exercise #1 – The NYSE First Trade chart

1. Where is the Asc located in this horoscope of the New York Stock Exchange?
2. Where is the MC located in this horoscope?
3. Which signs comprise the 10th House?

Please refer to the De-Brief section of this book for answers.

4. THE 18.6 YEAR BUSINESS CYCLE

McWhirter closely followed the economic forecasts of Colonel Leonard P. Ayers at the Cleveland Trust Company. Colonel Ayers was a devout student of the stock market and was revered by the American Government for his published correlations between business activity and stock market indices. One of his more famous correlations related the number of operating blast furnaces in the American steel industry to stock market tops and bottoms.

A further correlation was noted between American economic activity and astrology. Whether McWhirter was the one to identify this correlation or whether Ayers recognized it first remains unclear.

The correlation between economic activity and astrology posits that the North Node of the Moon moving through the various signs of the zodiac aligns to periods of strength and weakness in economic activity. A full journey of the North Node around the twelve signs of the zodiac comprises one complete business cycle in the economy. In today's age of globalization and Central Bank co-ordinations, the business cycle can be viewed on a global scale.

So, what exactly is the North Node of the Moon?

Earth and the other planets orbit around the Sun in a plane of motion called the *ecliptic plane*. The Moon meanwhile orbits the Earth in a plane of motion called the *lunar plane*. Mathematically, two planes that are not parallel must intersect each other. The points of intersection are called the North Node and the South Node.

The mathematical concept of the Nodes was first recognized thousands of years ago by ancient Hindu astrologers who called the North Node *rahu* and the South Node *ketu.* In any horoscope chart, the North and South Nodes are 180 degrees opposite one another. Therefore, it is only necessary to study the position of one of the Nodes. McWhirter and Ayers focused only on the North Node. In fact, modern astrologers today also focus mainly on the North Node.

The North Node is deemed to have dampening, suppressive forces similar to that of Saturn. So, at the peak of a business cycle, these dampening forces are at a minimum and at the low point in a busiress cycle these dampening forces are at their strongest.

The simple diagram in Figure 3 illustrates the intersection of the ecliptic and lunar planes.

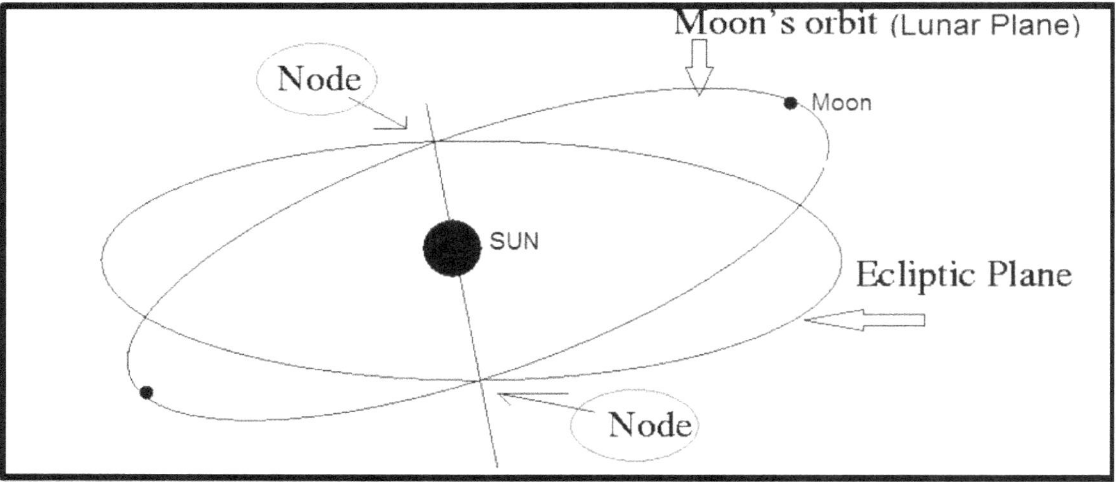

Figure 3 The Nodes

Mathematically, to an observer positioned on Earth, it appears as though the Nodes are progressing backwards in a retrograde motion as illustrated in Figure 4. The length of time for the Nodes to pass through the twelve zodiac signs is 18.6 years. This means that every 1.55 years, the Nodes will enter into a different zodiac sign.

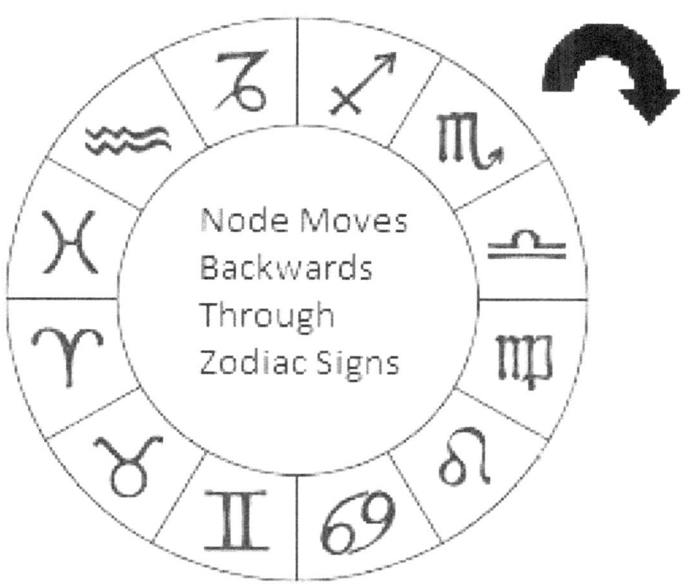

Figure 4 – Retrograde Node Movement

Using economic data from Colonel Ayers at the Cleveland Trust Company, McWhirter was able to discern the following:

- As the Node enters Aquarius, the low point of economic activity has been reached.
- As the Node leaves Aquarius and begins to transit through Capricorn and Sagittarius, the economy starts its return to more normal levels of activity.
- As the Node passes through Scorpio and Libra, the economy is functioning at above normal.
- As the Node transits through Leo, the high point in economic activity has been reached.
- As the Node transits through Cancer and Gemini, the economy is easing back towards normal.
- As the Node enters the sign of Taurus, the economy begins to slow.
- As the Node enters Aquarius, the low point of economic activity has been reached and a full 18.6 year cycle has been completed.

McWhirter further observed some secondary factors that can influence the tenor of economic activity in a good way, no matter which sign the Node is in at the time:

- Jupiter being 0 degrees conjunct to the Node
- Jupiter being in Gemini or Cancer
- Pluto being at a favorable (30, 60 or 120 degree) aspect to the Node

McWhirter also observed some secondary factors that can influence the tenor of economic activity in a bad way, no matter which sign the Node is in at the time:

- Saturn being 0, 90 or 180 degrees to the Node
- Saturn in Gemini or Cancer
- Uranus in Gemini
- Uranus being 0, 90 or 180 degrees to the Node
- Pluto being at an unfavorable (0, 90 or 180 degree) aspect to the Node

Summary Points

The North and South Nodes mathematically occur where the ecliptic plane intersects the lunar plane.

Astrologers focus almost exclusively on the North Node.

From our vantage point here on Earth, the North Node appears to be moving backwards through the twelve zodiac signs.

It takes ~1.55 years for the North Node to move through one entire zodiac sign.

In the McWhirter methodology, the economy is deemed to be at its low point when the North Node is moving through Aquarius. Economic researchers of a more recent date have extended this observation to include the real estate market.

The economy and real estate market will then improve, reaching a peak as the North Node passes through Leo.

The economy and real estate market will decline again, reaching a low point as the North Node transits through Aquarius to complete its 18.6 year cycle.

5. HISTORICAL NODE OCCURRENCES IN AQUARIUS

To further illustrate the correlation between the Node and the business cycle, consider the following examples of when the Node was passing through Aquarius:

Immediately prior to 1859, the American economy had come under duress with the failure of the Ohio Life Insurance and Trust Company. In addition, bankers on Wall Street had over-extended themselves with massive lending to railway companies seeking to profit from the masses of settlers heading west. In early 1859, the Node moved into Aquarius which signalled the low point in an economic cycle. The Node was 90 degrees square Uranus as well which meant the tenor of the cycle was further negatively influenced. Economic slowdowns can irritate and polarize people. In London, Karl Marx penned *A Contribution to the Critique of Political Economy* (the precursor to Das Kapital) in early 1859. In America, the issue of slavery was being hotly debated. No sooner had the Node transited out of Aquarius, than the Civil War began in the United States.

In April 1896, the Node transited into Aquarius and the American economy (along with commodity prices) slumped when investors thought the Gold Standard would be abolished.

In mid-July 1914, the Node was in the latter stages of Pisces, on its way towards Aquarius and a low point in the economic cycle, when World War I broke out.

In mid-1933, the Node was about to enter into Aquarius thus signalling a low point in the economic cycle. This time period marked the depths of the Great Depression.

In early 1952, the Node was about to enter the sign of Aquarius as America found itself engaged in war in Korea.

In late 1970, the Node was again poised to enter Aquarius. America was deeply embroiled in the Vietnam War. War was also raging on the Indian sub-continent. Inflation was posing a problem to the global economy. Energy prices were crimping the North American economy. Tensions were rising between Arabs and Israelis in the Middle East.

In May 1989, the Node was again ready to enter Aquarius. Inflation was hurting the economy. In America, the Savings and Loans crisis was reaching a crescendo. Economic growth was low and tensions were again rising in the Middle East. Coalition forces would soon become engaged in Operation Desert Storm in response to Iraq having invaded its neighbor Kuwait.

In early 2008, the Node was again on the doorstep of the sign of Aquarius. As it entered Aquarius, it made a 0 degree aspect to Uranus. The completion of this particular 18.6 year economic cycle would be a harsh one with the entire capitalist system coming under extreme duress.

Summary Points

The North Node in Aquarius can result in much more than just an economic low point. The North Node in Aquarius can lead to war, inflation, stock market corrections and political strife.

6. THE CURRENT ECONOMIC CYCLE

The current 18.6 year economic cycle can be examined using the North Node.   The horoscope in Figure 5 illustrates the planetary positions at December 31 of 2007.

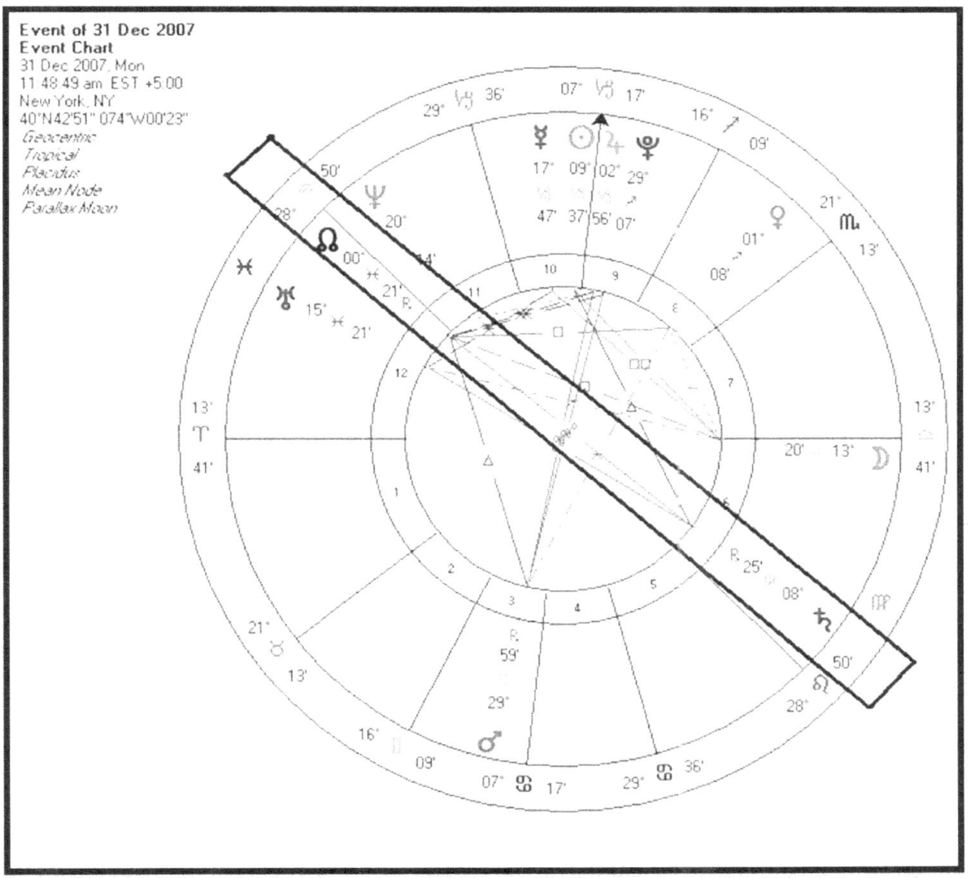

Figure 5 – Planetary Positions at December 31, 2007

Observe that at December 31, 2007 the North Node was at 0 degrees of Pisces and would next be moving into Aquarius where it would spend 1.55 years. In the McWhirter approach, the Node in Aquarius marks the low point of economic activity. We can also see the position of Saturn at 180 degrees opposite the Node. McWhirter cautioned that such hard aspects between Saturn and the Node can negatively influence the tenor of economic activity. We now know with the benefit of hindsight that the economic downturn that followed the Node moving into Aquarius in opposition to Saturn was a severe one. For many of us, this was the most severe economic downturn we may ever see in our lifetimes.

The daily price chart in Figure 6 illustrates the price performance of the Dow Jones Average during this timeframe.

Figure 6 – Dow Jones daily chart August 2007 to January 2008

Note that the Dow had reached its peak in early October 2007 - about 10 weeks prior to the Node making its transition into Aquarius at the end of December 2007. Alert investors following the McWhirter methodology would have been re-organizing their portfolios or even exiting the stock market completely.

Many people have asked me if the McWhirter methodology is unique to the USA or if it can be seen globally. The answer is - globally.

Figure 7 – Weekly chart FTSE 100 Index

The weekly price chart in Figure 7 illustrates the price performance of the FTSE 100 Index in Great Britain at the time the Node was transitioning into Aquarius. Note that the FTSE 100 Index peaked in late 2007 around the same time as the S&P500 Index. Great Britain then also experienced a dramatic slowdown in its economic activity as the Node moved through Aquarius. McWhirter notes that as the Node transits Capricorn, the economy will start to recover. The horoscope in Figure 8 illustrates planetary positions in February 2009. At that time, the Node was at 8 degrees of Aquarius and would soon be moving out of that sign and into Capricorn. Interestingly, at that time Jupiter was in Aquarius and was nearing a 0 degree conjunction with the Node.

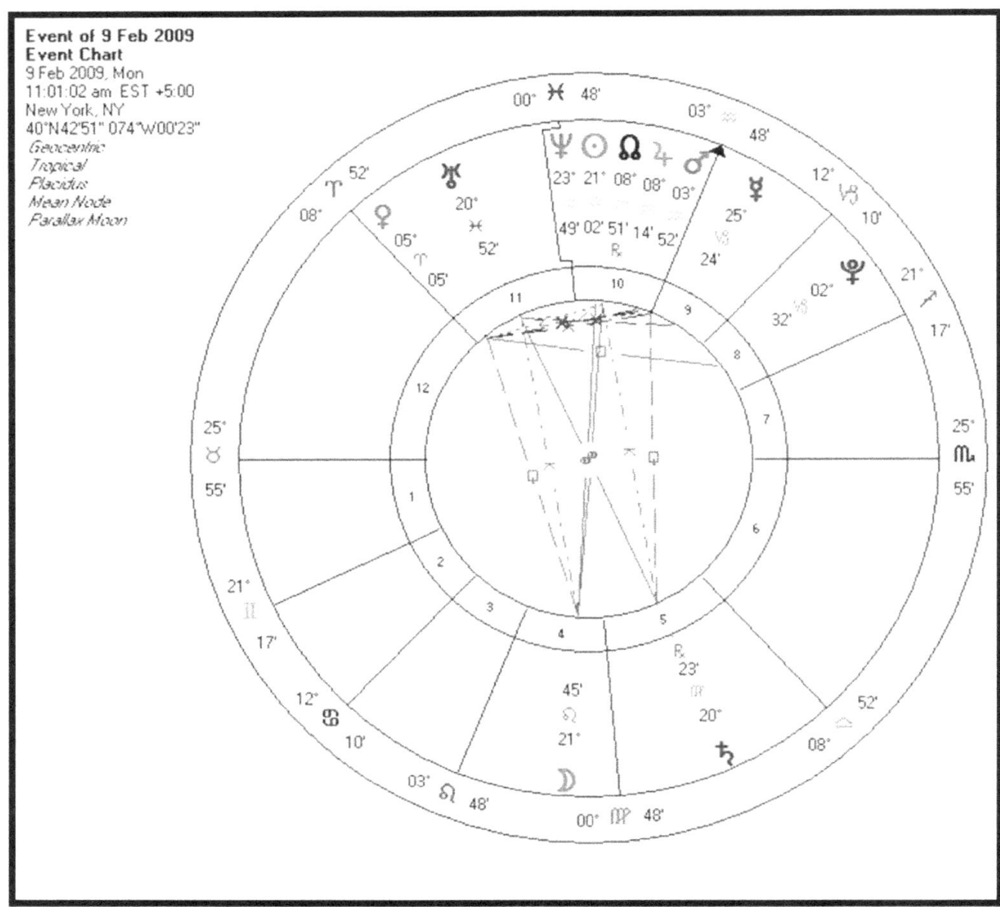

Figure 8 – Planetary Positions February 2009

McWhirter notes that Jupiter being conjunct to Node can positively influence the tenor of the economic cycle. We further know in hindsight that North American stock markets along with many global stock markets bottomed in March 2009. So too did real estate markets around the globe. By late July 2009, the Node had transitioned into Capricorn and economies around the globe were showing signs of wanting to slowly mend thanks also in part to some quantitative easing assistance from Central Bankers.

But, this mending process would not be all smooth sailing. The horoscope in Figure 9 shows the planetary positions at May 2010.

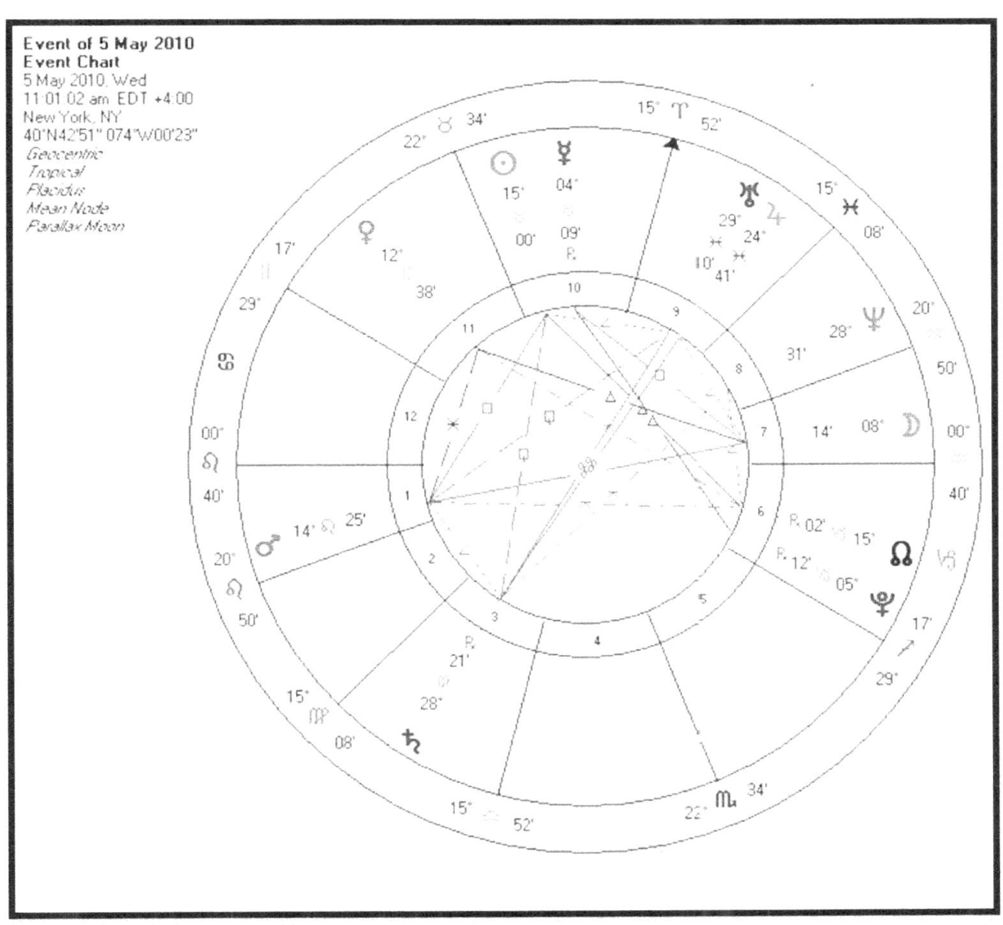

Figure 9 – Planetary Positions May 2010

Note in this horoscope that Node and Pluto are separated by 10 degrees in the sign of Capricorn. By November 2010, Node and Pluto would be separated by 0 degrees to form an exact conjunction. In the McWhirter approach, such hard aspects of Node and Pluto can weigh negatively on the tenor of the economic cycle. We now know this was in fact the case. Furthermore, from August through late October 2010, the Node was making a hard 90 degree aspect to Saturn. In the McWhirter approach, such hard aspects between Node and Saturn can weigh negatively on the tenor of the economic cycle.

As the astrology was suggesting, the economy was not recovering as robustly as it should have been. It needed more help. That help came from the Federal Reserve in November 2010 when Ben Bernanke announced the implementation of a second round of quantitative easing dubbed 'QE2'.

With the aid of QE2, the economy slowly continued to recover, but there were still headwinds. The Node-Pluto conjunction referred to in Figure 9 was still active and would remain so until March 2011. From late November 2010 to mid-April 2011, the Node was also making a hard 90 degree aspect to Uranus. Contributing as well to the headwinds was the Saturn-Uranus 180 degree opposition which would run its course by August, 2011.

In the Autumn of 2012 as the Node was in Sagittarius, the Federal Reserve announced another round of Quantitative Easing in which it would buy a total of $80 billion a month of mortgage related securities. The timing of this move was prudent as the North Node still had one more hurdle to cross in 2013 From late June 2013 to early November 2013, the Node would be making a zero degree conjunction with Saturn. After this Saturn conjunction, there would be no further negative aspects until a Node-Uranus 180 degree event late in 2014. Accordingly, in June 2013, the Fed started hinting strongly that sometime later in 2013 the economy would be strong enough to run on a lesser amount of monthly stimulus. This Fed hint came just as Jupiter moved into the sign of Cancer. The McWhirter approach dictates that Jupiter in Cancer is a positive influence on the tenor of the economic cycle. In December 2013 as Ben Bernanke was about to wrap up his term as Fed Governor, the first stimulus tapering was announced.

This brief narrative almost makes us wonder if the Federal Reserve is aware of the McWhirter methodology and has used it to guide their stimulus program decisions.

In April 2014 the Node completed its journey through Scorpio and entered Libra. In the McWhirter methodology, the Node in Libra marks a further strengthening of the economy. Jupiter will finally leave Cancer in July 2014. As this manuscript is being readied for printing, Fed Governor Janet Yellen is on record as saying there is a wide array of data that must be examined as part of Fed decision making. In other words, she is uncertain if the economy can withstand a small hike in the key Federal Reserve interest rate. And rightly so, with a Node-Uranus 180 degree aspect looming at the end of 2014 and a Node-Pluto 90 degree hard aspect coming shortly after.

Looking farther ahead, watch also for Node to make a 90 degree square to Saturn between March and November, 2016. The high point in this current North Node 18.6 year economic cycle will occur in April 2017-October 2018 as Node moves through Leo .

Summary Points

North American markets (as well as many international markets) bottomed in March 2009 as the Node was nearing the end of its transit through Aquarius.

The current economic cycle will remain in a positive growth mode until 2017-2018 after which time it will begin to moderate.

For a more in-depth treatment of economic cycles, it is suggested that one reference the works of U.K. economist Fred Harrison. Mr. Harrison stops just shy of using the word astrology in his works, but he clearly identifies what he calls an 18 year economic cycle, the beginnings of which he traces back to the time around the Industrial Revolution.

7. FORECASTING INFLECTION POINTS ON THE NEW YORK STOCK EXCHANGE

The McWhirter methodology extends to forecasting price inflection points on the New York Stock Exchange. At the time McWhirter was publishing her work, the Dow Jones Average was the main index used to quantify price action on the New York Stock Exchange. Today, there are many different indices used to track activity on the New York Exchange – the S&P500 being a main one. However, the Dow Jones Average continues to be a widely followed index. In keeping with McWhirter's work, I have thus decided to structure many of the examples in this manuscript around the Dow Jones Average.

A *lunar cycle* is the time it takes for the Moon to completely orbit the Earth. A lunar cycle is 29.5 days. A lunar cycle begins at a New Moon and ends 29.5 days later at the next New Moon.

The McWhirter technique for identifying inflection points on the New York Stock Exchange involves examining the position of planets in the zodiac wheel at the time of a New Moon. Hard aspects between the New Moon and planets such as Mars, Saturn and Uranus can be a harbinger of a volatile lunar cycle to come. During a lunar cycle, it is also important to watch as the Moon transits past Mars and Neptune, the co-rulers of the 10th House in the New York Stock Exchange First Trade chart as well as any planets that were present in the 10th House at the time of the New Moon.

The psychological theory behind this method is that the Moon has a strong effect on human emotion. As the Moon passes by these key planetary locations of the zodiac wheel, there is a very high probability that the New York Stock Exchange will exhibit a trend change. One must also watch planets such as Venus, Mercury and Mars as they transit past these key locations. The scientific basis for the Moon triggering emotional responses at these key locations remains a mystery to this author. Hopefully in years to come scientists and psychologists who are exploring the field of *cosmo-biology* will propse some answers.

As an interesting exercise, pay attention to your own mood swings. Do you feel different during a New Moon versus a Full Moon?

The McWhirter method for forecasting inflection points also takes into account the position of the Ascendant and the Mid-Heaven in the horoscope chart of the New York Stock Exchange on May 17, 1792. This horoscope chart is referred to in the remainder of this publication as the *natal birth chart* of the New York Stock Exchange. The Ascendant point is at 14 degrees Cancer and the Mid-Heaven point was at 24 degrees Pisces in this natal birth chart. Figure 10 illustrates this natal birth chart. So, why would the original founders of the New York Stock Exchange arrange it so that the Exchange commenced business on May 17 at a time when the Ascendant was at 14 degrees of Cancer? The answer may rest with the date the United States came into being. On July 4, 1776, the Sun was at 14 degrees of Cancer. Saturn was also in the 10th House.

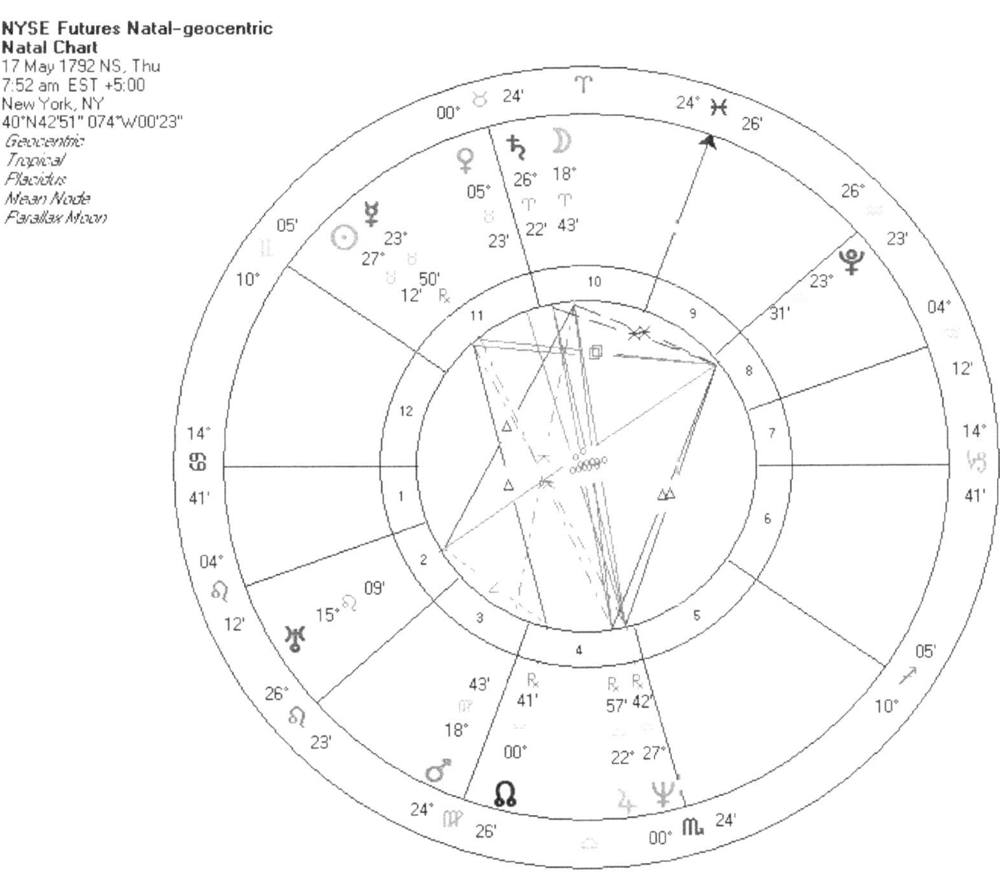

Figure 10 – NYSE natal birth chart

8.   SOFTWARE AND EPHEMERIS TABLES

To employ the McWhirter method most efficiently, one should use a software program that allows the user to progress the Moon around the zodiac wheel with the click of a mouse. One such software program is Solar Fire Gold. It retails for approximately US$360 at www.alabe.com.

In the absence of a software program, it is still possible to use the McWhirter method by manually preparing a horoscope wheel showing planetary placements. After all, there was no software programs in 1937 when the McWhirter method was first pioneered.

To assist you with manually constructing zodiac wheels, you can make photocopies of the blank zodiac wheel contained in the Appendix to this Study Guide.

If not using a software program to determine planetary placements, you can find the planetary positions in a Geocentric Ephemeris.

Most bookstores sell Ephemeris books. A good one is *The New American Ephemeris for the 21st Century*, authored by Enrique Pottenger.

It is also possible to find Ephemeris tables on line. One reliable website is http://www.astro.com.

9. INFLECTION POINT CASE STUDIES - NYSE

The Asian Currency Crisis

For a brief time in 1997, the global economy was gripped with fear as currencies of several Asian nations slumped in value in response to a shift in interest rate policy in the USA. In the month of August 1997, a New Moon occurred on August 3rd. At this New Moon, the positions of the planets were:

Sun	11 Leo
Moon	11 Leo
North Node	21 Virgo
Mercury	8 Virgo
Venus	12 Virgo
Mars	23 Libra
Jupiter	17 Aquarius
Saturn	20 Aries
Uranus	6 Aquarius
Neptune	28 Capricorn
Pluto	2 Sagittarius

Using your software program, generate the horoscope chart for the date of August 3, 1997 using Placidus house divisions. Shift the Placidus house divisions around by moving the Ascendant until the cusp of the first house is at 14 degrees of Cancer.

Your resulting horoscope should look like the zodiac wheel in Figure 11 which has been prepared with Solar Fire Gold.

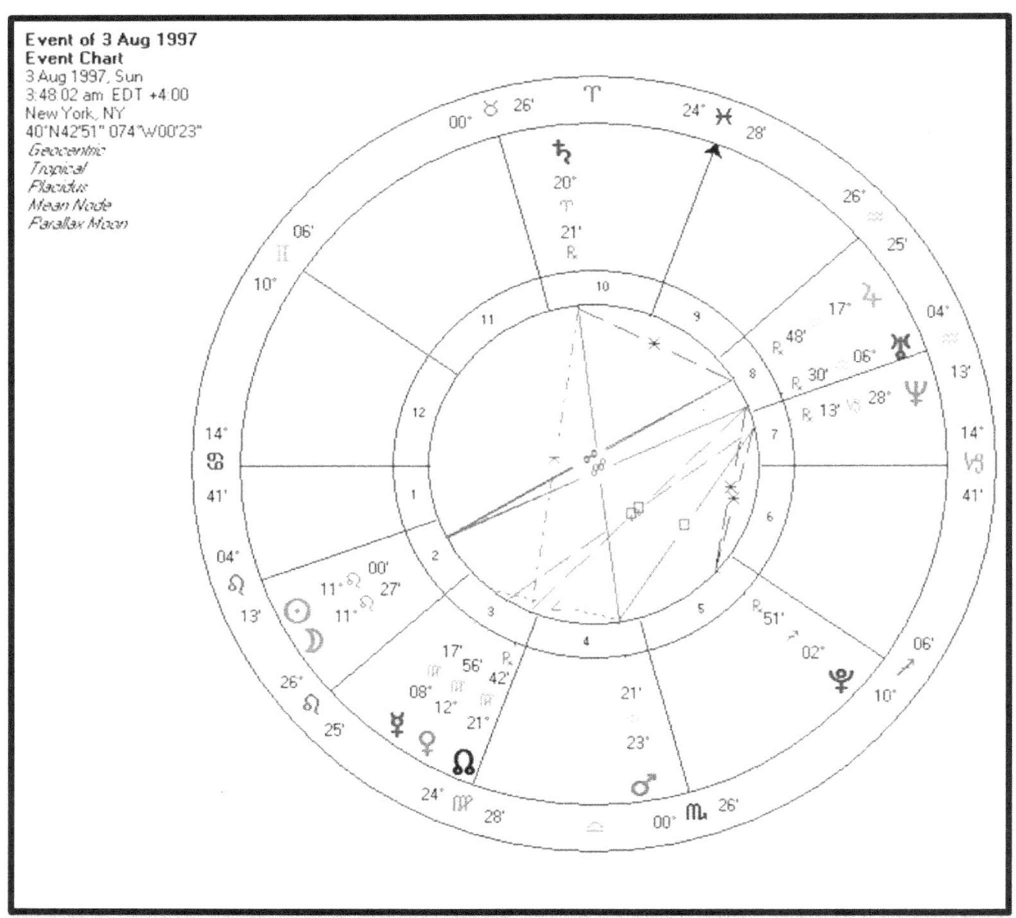

Figure 11 Planetary Positions August 1997

Step 1: Are there any planets in the 10th House?

We can see that Saturn is in the 10th House. Saturn has a reputation as an oppressive planet and to see it in the 10th House is suggestive of some volatility on the New York Stock Exchange in the lunar cycle to come.

Step 2: Is the New Moon at either the Mid-Heaven (24 Pisces) or the Ascendant (14 Cancer) of the New York Stock Exchange?

The New Moon is not at either of these key locations.

Step 3: Is the New Moon at an unfavorable aspect to Mars or Neptune? (These planets are the co-rulers of the natal birth chart of the New York Stock Exchange).

The New Moon makes no aspects to Mars or Neptune

Step 4: Are any of the outer planets at aspects to Mars or Neptune?

Saturn makes a 180 degree hard aspect to Mars, suggesting some difficulties on the New York Stock Exchange in the lunar cycle ahead.

Step 5: Are Saturn and Uranus at an aspect to one another?

Saturn and Uranus are not in aspect to one another

Step 6: Does the New Moon make any aspects to Jupiter, Saturn, Neptune, Uranus or Pluto?

The New Moon makes a 180 degree aspect to Jupiter and Uranus. Uranus is a planet that suggests change in a negative way. Jupiter suggests expansion. Having the lunation opposite both these planets suggests a lunar cycle that will be volatile as positive and negative forces fight it out.

When looking for aspect angles in a horoscope chart, note that it is not necessary for the angles to be precise. McWhirter uses the following rules for aspect angles:

McWhirter Rules for Aspect Angles

1. In the case of a 0 degree conjunction 180 degree opposition, it is acceptable to have planets within 10 degrees of being opposite to each other.

2. In the case of a 90 degree square, it is acceptable to have planets within 5 degrees of being square to each other.

3. In the case of a 60 degree sextile aspect, it is acceptable to have planets within 5 degrees of being sextile to each other.

4. In the case of a 30 degree semi-sextile aspect, it is acceptable to have planets within 3 degrees of being semi-sextile to each oteher.

5. In the case of a 120 degree trine aspect, it is acceptable to have planets within 5 degrees of being trine to each other

Analysis: What are the dates when the Moon transits past key planets and key locations?

Having identified key aspects in steps 2 through 6, the transit of the Moon can now be watched. Using your software program, advance the Moon around the zodiac wheel to see when it passes by the key aspect points identified in steps 2 through 6.

The chart in Figure 12 illustrates the price action of the Dow during August 2007 lunar cycle.

- Moon transited past Mars on August 9, a Saturday. The day before, Friday, saw an inflection point on the Dow at just over 13,740.

- On the 16th-17th of August, Moon transited past Uranus and Neptune. The Dow recorded a swing bottom from the 12,550 level in harmony with these transits. The 18th was also a Full Moon which no doubt also contributed to the reversal.

- On August 21st, Moon transited past Saturn and the very next day the Dow responded by breaking out above the highs of the previous 3 trading sessions.

- On the 28th the Moon transited past the 14 Cancer Ascendant position and the Dow recorded a nasty 200 point sell-off.

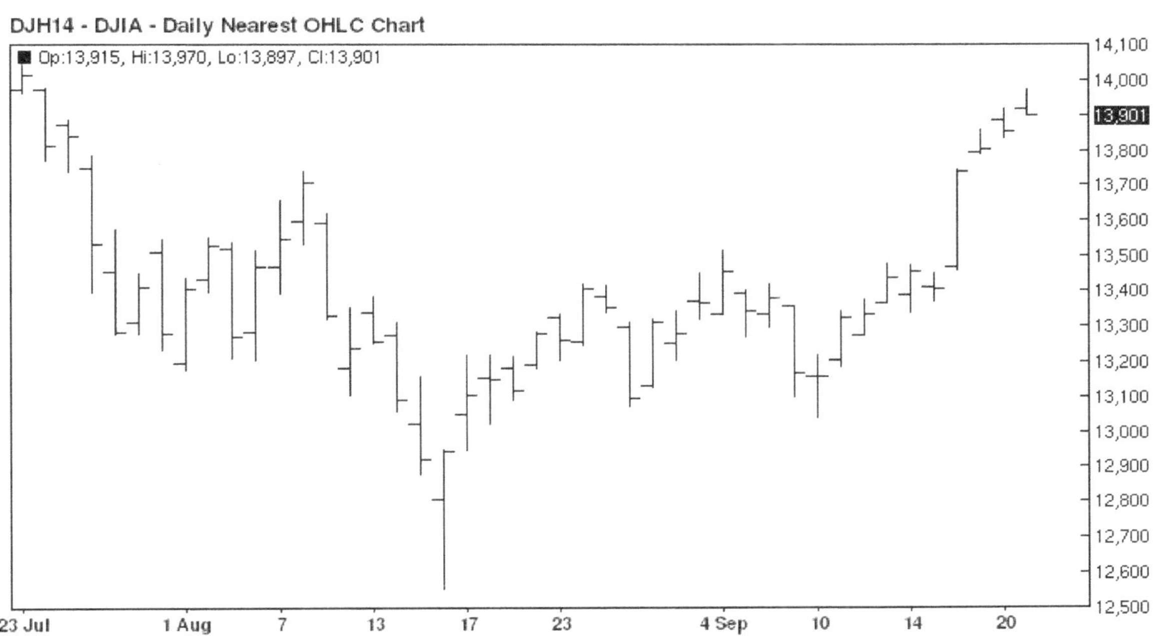

Figure 12 - Daily chart Dow Jones Average July through September 2007

The Market Top in 2000

The Dow Jones reached a peak in the month of January, 2000. The New Moon occurred on January 6th. At this New Moon, the positions of the planets were:

Sun	15 Capricorn
Moon	16 Capricorn
North Node	4 Leo
Mercury	10 Capricorn
Venus	8 Sagittarius
Mars	2 Pisces
Jupiter	25 Aries
Saturn	10 Taurus
Uranus	15 Aquarius
Neptune	3 Aquarius
Pluto	11 Sagittarius

Using your software program, generate the horoscope chart for the date of January 6, 2000 using Placidus house divisions. Shift the Placidus house divisions around until the cusp of the first house is at 14 degrees of Cancer.

Your resulting horoscope should look like the zodiac wheel in Figure 13 which has been prepared with Solar Fire Gold.

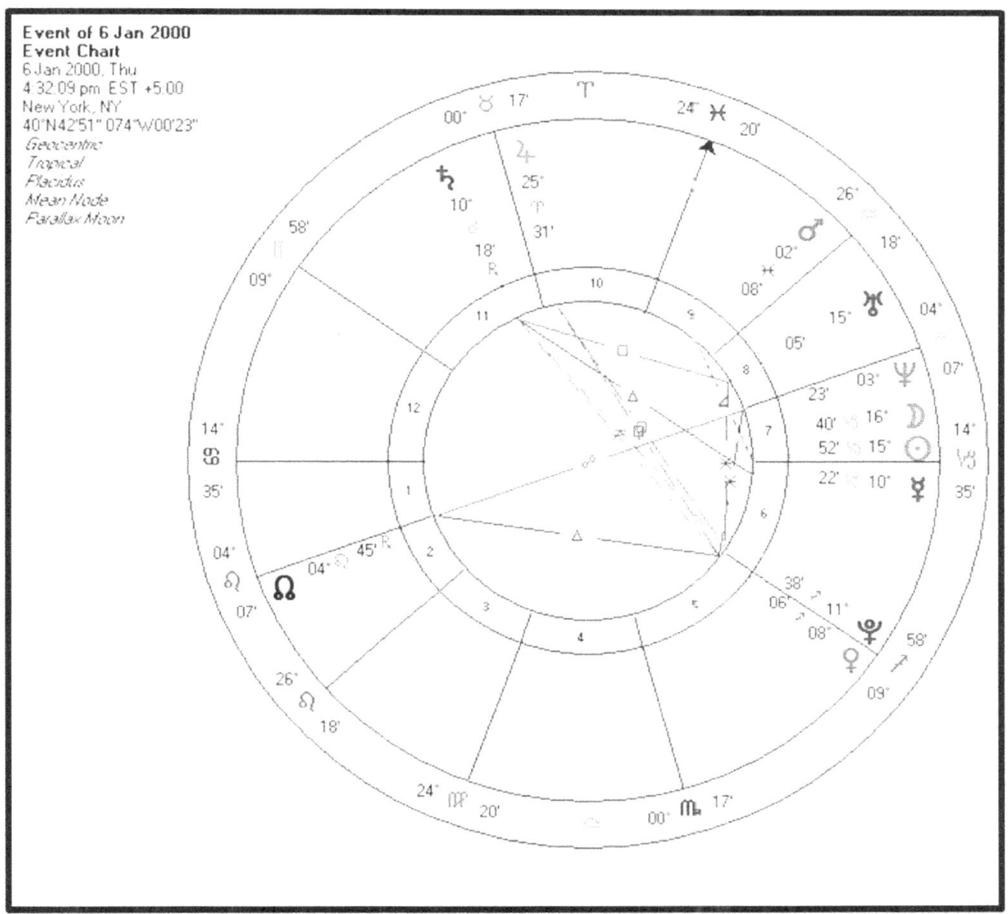

Figure 13 – Planetary Positions January 2000

Step 1: Are there any planets in the 10th House?

Jupiter is in the 10th House.

Step 2: Is the New Moon at either the Mid-Heaven (24 Pisces) or the Ascendant (14 Cancer) of the New York Stock Exchange?

The New Moon is 180 degrees opposite to the Ascendant position of 14 Cancer. This hard aspect suggests that caution is warranted in the coming lunar cycle.

Step 3: Is the New Moon at an unfavorable aspect to Mars or Neptune?

The New Moon is at a 45 degree hard aspect to Mars. Aspects of 45 degrees, although difficult, tend to be less difficult than 0, 90 or 180 degree aspects. Nevertheless, some caution is warranted.

Step 4: Are any of the outer planets in aspect to Mars or Neptune?

There are no planets in aspect. However, it must be noted that the Node is 180 degrees opposite to Neptune which is a further suggestion that caution is warranted.

Step 5: Are Saturn and Uranus at an aspect to one another?

Saturn is 5 degrees away from making a 90 degree square to Uranus. This is another red flag.

Step 6: Does the New Moon make any aspects to Jupiter, Saturn, Neptune, Uranus or Pluto?

The New Moon is just within orb of being 120 degrees to Saturn.

Based on the above analysis, we can conclude that Mars, Node, Saturn, Neptune and Uranus are all key positions to be alert to during the coming lunar cycle.

Analysis: What are the dates when the Moon transits past key planets and key locations?

- The daily chart in Figure 14 illustrates the price action of the Dow Jones during the January 2000 lunar cycle.

- The Dow enjoyed an up-day on the 7th as Moon passed by Neptune.

- From the 10th to the 13th, the Dow consolidated sideways, despite Moon passing by Mars and the Mid Heaven locations.

- On the 14th, the Moon passed by Jupiter in the 10th House. Although it was not immediately recognized at that moment, this passage of this key location would be the market top for a good while to come.

-

- The very next day (Saturday), Moon would pass by heavyweight Saturn and the fate of the market would be carved in stone.

- The 19th saw critical support levels broken as Moon passed by the 14 Cancer Ascendant point.

- The 21st saw more downward pressure as Moon passed by the Node location at 4 Leo.

- From the 23rd through the 27th, the Dow consolidated sideways as Moon was not making any aspects.

- From the 31st to February 4th, the Dow attempted to rally as Moon passed Neptune, but it was too late – the damage had been done. And more damage was soon to follow with the New Moon on February 5th.

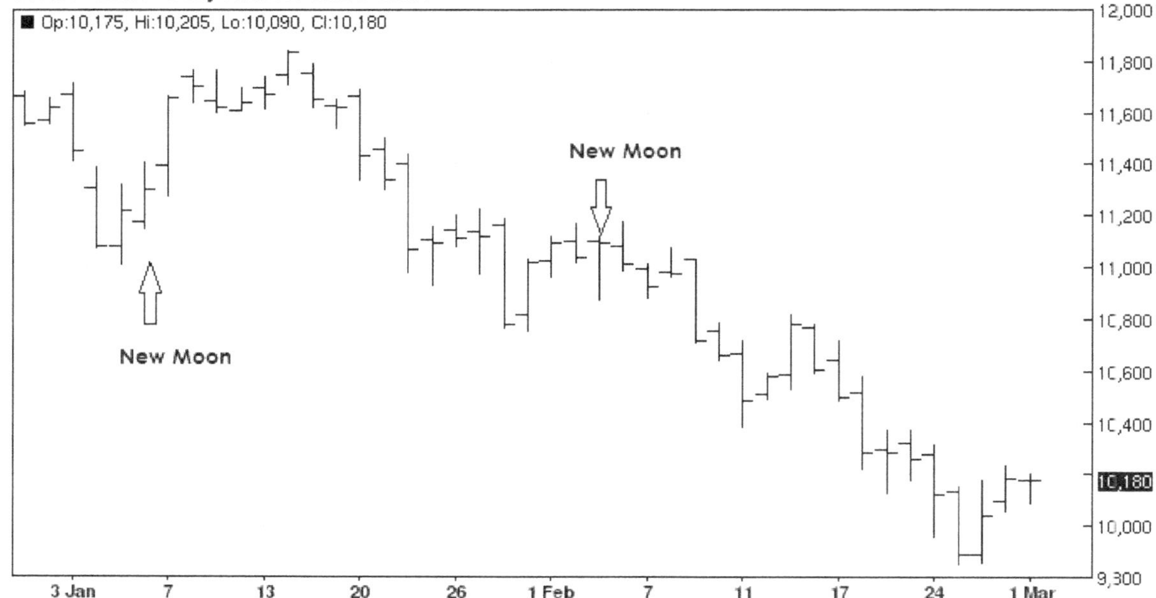

Figure 14 – Daily nearest chart of Dow Jones for January 2000

The Market Low in 2002

North American financial markets made a significant low in October 2002 much to the relief of weary, beaten-up investors. The New Moon in October 2002 occurred on October 6th. At this New Moon, the positions of the planets were:

Sun	13 Libra
Moon	23 Libra
North Node	11 Gemini
Mercury	28 Virgo
Venus	15 Scorpio
Mars	24 Virgo
Jupiter	13 Leo
Saturn	29 Gemini
Uranus	25 Aquarius
Neptune	8 Aquarius
Pluto	15 Sagittarius

Using your software program, generate the horoscope chart for the date of October 6, 2002 using Placidus house divisions. Shift the Placidus house divisions around until the cusp of the first house is at 14 degrees of Cancer.

Your resulting horoscope should look like the zodiac wheel in Figure 15 which has been prepared with Solar Fire Gold.

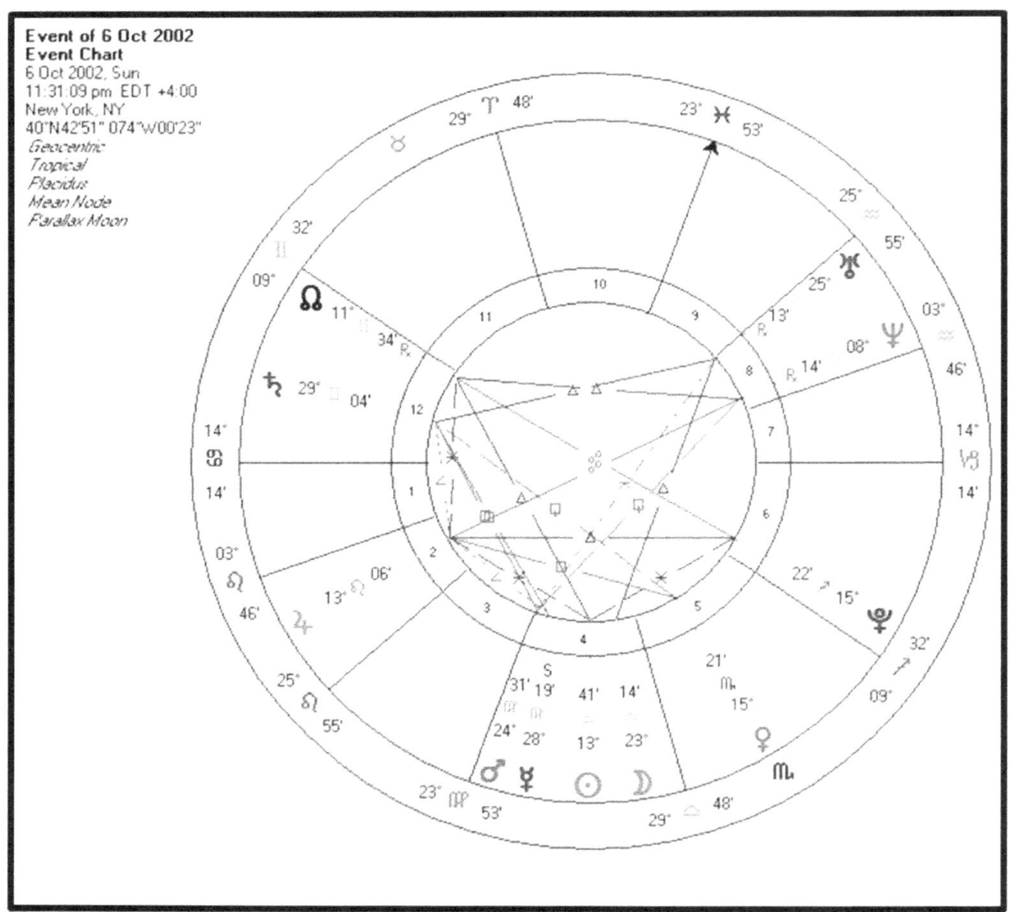

Figure 15 – Planetary Positions October 2002

Step 1: Are there any planets in the 10th House?

There are no planets in the 10th House.

Step 2: Is the New Moon at either the Mid-Heaven (24 Pisces) or the Ascendant (14 Cancer) of the New York Stock Exchange?

The New Moon is not conjunct either of these key locations.

Step 3: Is the New Moon at an unfavorable aspect to Mars or Neptune?

The New Moon is at 115 degrees to Neptune. This just qualifies as a favorable 120 degree trine aspect under the McWhirter rules for aspects.

Step 4: Do any of the outer planets make aspects to Mars or Neptune?

Jupiter makes a 45 degree aspect to Mars, Saturn is 90 degrees to Mars, Uranus is 150 degrees to Mars, Neptune is 135 degrees to Mars. In addition, the Node is a favorable 120 degrees to Neptune.

Step 5: Are Saturn and Uranus at an aspect to one another?

Saturn is 120 degrees trine to Uranus. This is a favorable occurrence and warrants some attention.

Step 6: Does the New Moon make any aspects to Jupiter, Saturn, Neptune, Uranus or Pluto?

The New Moon makes a favorable 60 degree aspect to Pluto, a favorable 120 degree aspect to the Node and a favorable 60 degree aspect to Jupiter. This suggests a coming lunar cycle that should have some positive features to it.

Based on the above, we can conclude that Saturn, Jupiter, Pluto, Neptune, Node and Uranus are all key positions to be alert to during the month of October.

Analysis: What are the dates when the Moon transits past key planets and key locations?

The daily chart in Figure 16 illustrates the price action of the Dow Jones Average during October 2002.

- The Moon transited past Pluto on the 10th of October and a trend change resulted. Although it was perhaps suspected by some traders at the time, this trend change was in fact the end of the nasty downturn that had begun back in March 2000. From this low, the Dow began to recover smartly.

- The Moon passed Neptune, Uranus and the Mid-Heaven positions over the next 7 days, with many of the trading sessions delivering powerful surges higher.

- October 24th saw a stiff drop as Moon passed the Node position. This drop partly reversed itself the next day as Moon passed by Saturn's location.

- A few days later - October 29th saw a 180 point drop and then a complete intra-day reversal as Moon transited past the Jupiter location.

- As the lunar cycle drew to a close, the Moon passing Mars led to a continuation of the rally.

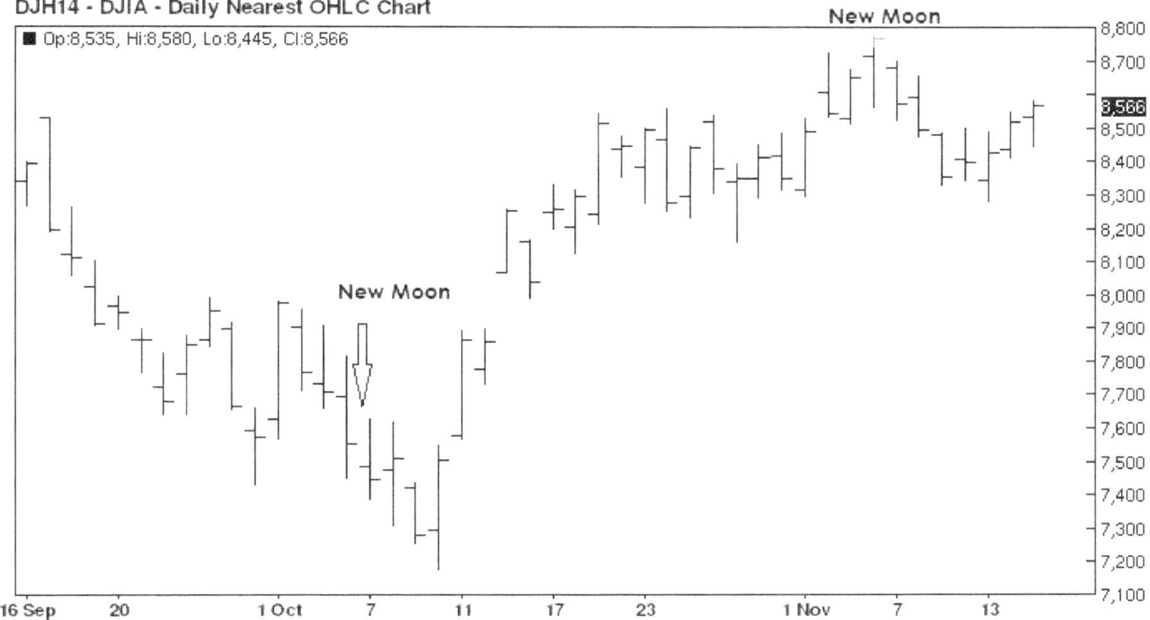

Figure 16 – Daily chart Dow Jones October 2002

The Market High in 2007

The Dow Jones made a high in October 2007. But, the New Moon occurred on October 11th. How then does one account for the first 10 days of October?

The McWhirter methodology is based on the 29.5 days of a lunar cycle, not on the 30 or 31 days of a calendar month. This example very adeptly illustrates this point. To properly account for the first 10 days of October, it is necessary to extend this case study to also include the New Moon that occurred on September 11th. At the September 11th New Moon, the positions of the planets were:

Sun	18 Virgo
Moon	14 Virgo
North Node	6 Pisces
Mercury	8 Libra
Venus	16 Leo
Mars	21 Gemini
Jupiter	11 Sagittarius
Saturn	1 Virgo
Uranus	16 Pisces
Neptune	19 Aquarius
Pluto	26 Sagittarius

Using your software program, generate the horoscope chart for the date of September 11, 2007 using Placidus house divisions. Shift the Placidus house divisions around until the cusp of the first house is at 14 degrees of Cancer.

Your resulting horoscope should look like the zodiac wheel in Figure 17 which has been prepared with Solar Fire Gold.

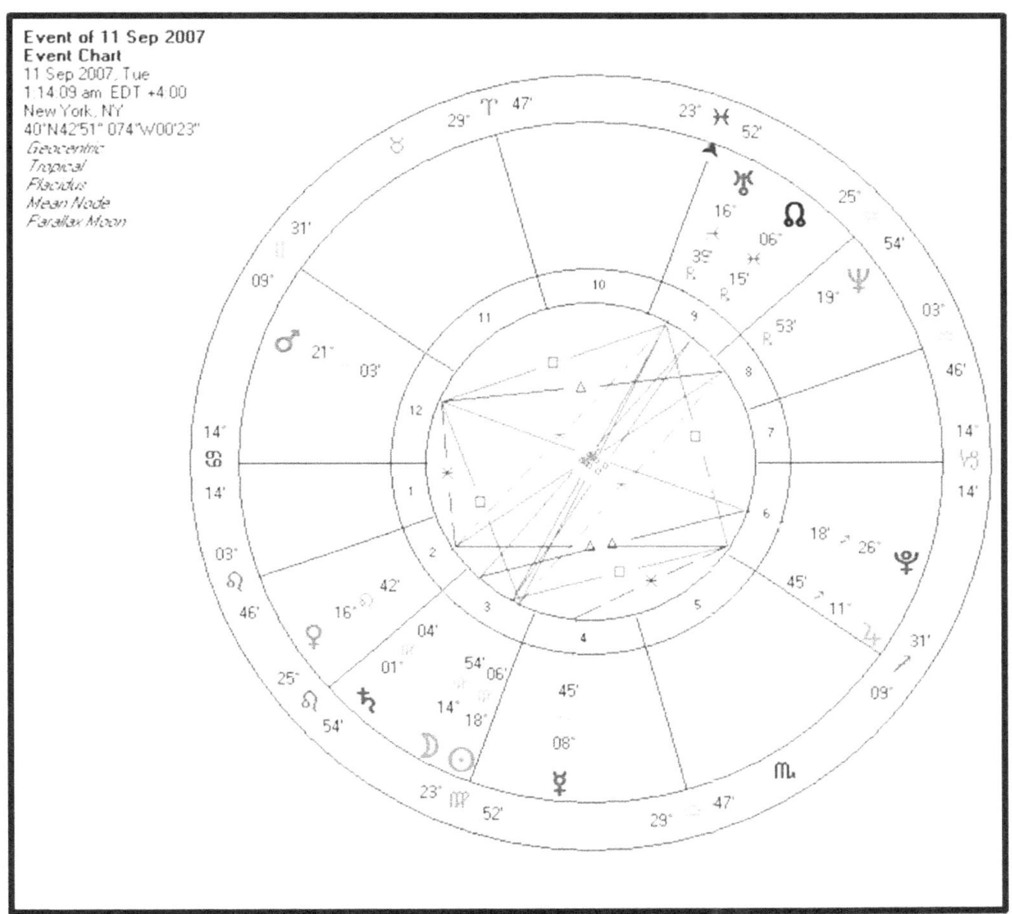

Figure 17 – Planetary Positions September 2007

Step 1: Are there any planets in the 10th House?

There are no planets in the 10th House.

Step 2: Is the New Moon at either the Mid-Heaven (24 Pisces) or the Ascendant (14 Cancer) of the New York Stock Exchange?

The New Moon is not conjunct either of these key locations.

Step 3: Is the New Moon at an unfavorable aspect to Mars or Neptune?

The New Moon is 90 degrees square to Mars. This square aspect to Mars is an occurrence that warrants attention.

Step 4: Do any of the outer planets make aspects to Mars or Neptune?

Uranus is at a hard 90 degrees square to Mars. Neptune is a favorable 120 degrees trine to its co-ruler Mars. Pluto is a hard 180 degrees opposite Mars. Mars is evidently quite a popular planet at this time. This warrants some caution as it implies a lunar cycle in which the forces of positive and negative may fight it out with Mars as the center of attention.

Step 5: Are Saturn and Uranus at an aspect to one another?

Saturn is not in aspect to Uranus. However, Saturn is opposite Node which implies that Saturn could be a key feature to watch in the coming lunar cycle.

Step 6: Does the New Moon make any aspects to Jupiter, Saturn, Neptune, Uranus or Pluto?

The New Moon makes a hard 90 degree square to Jupiter and a 180 degree hard aspect to Uranus. These hard aspects in the absence of any favorable aspects, warrant caution.

Based on the above, we can conclude that Mars, Uranus and Jupiter and Neptune are key positions to be alert to during the lunar cycle.

Analysis: What are the dates when the Moon transits past key planets and key locations?

The daily chart in Figure 19 illustrates the price action of the Dow Jones Average during September 2007.

- The market uptrend that had been ongoing continued in September, 2007. On the 18th as Moon transited past Jupiter, the Dow enjoyed a big up-day, rallying 250 points.

- On the 24th, the Moon passed by Neptune creating a small sell-off. The transit of Uranus on the 25th caused a swing bottom and a recovery in momentum.

- The transit past the Mid-Heaven position (24 Pisces) on the 26th moved the Dow slightly higher as it tested new highs.

- The uptrend added a further 160 points on the 1st of October as Moon approached Mars. The Dow eased off slightly on the 2nd as Moon passed by Mars.

- On the 3rd-4th of October, the Moon passed by the 14 of Cancer Ascendant point and the Dow eased a bit further. With this sensitive transit complete, the very next day – October 5th - delivered a push higher and a re-test of the October 1st highs.

- Moon passed Saturn on the 7th of October, a Sunday with no effect on the Dow Jones. When markets re-opened the next day, all was quiet.

- On the 9th, Moon made a 90 degree square to Pluto and the Dow increased its reach even further, gaining another 100 points. Within two days, the lunar cycle would be complete and the atmosphere on Wall Street would take on a very different feel.

The September New Moon has helped describe the events of early October. Now it is necessary to examine the October New Moon for clues as to the rest of October. At the October 11th New Moon, the positions of the planets were:

Sun	17 Libra
Moon	16 Libra
North Node	4 Pisces
Mercury	9 Scorpio
Venus	2 Virgo
Mars	5 Cancer
Jupiter	15 Sagittarius
Saturn	4 Virgo
Uranus	15 Pisces
Neptune	19 Aquarius
Pluto	26 Sagittarius

Using your software program, generate the horoscope chart for the date of October 11, 2007 using Placidus house divisions. Shift the Placidus house divisions around until the cusp of the first house is at 14 degrees of Cancer.

Your resulting horoscope should look like the zodiac wheel in Figure 18 which has been prepared with Solar Fire Gold.

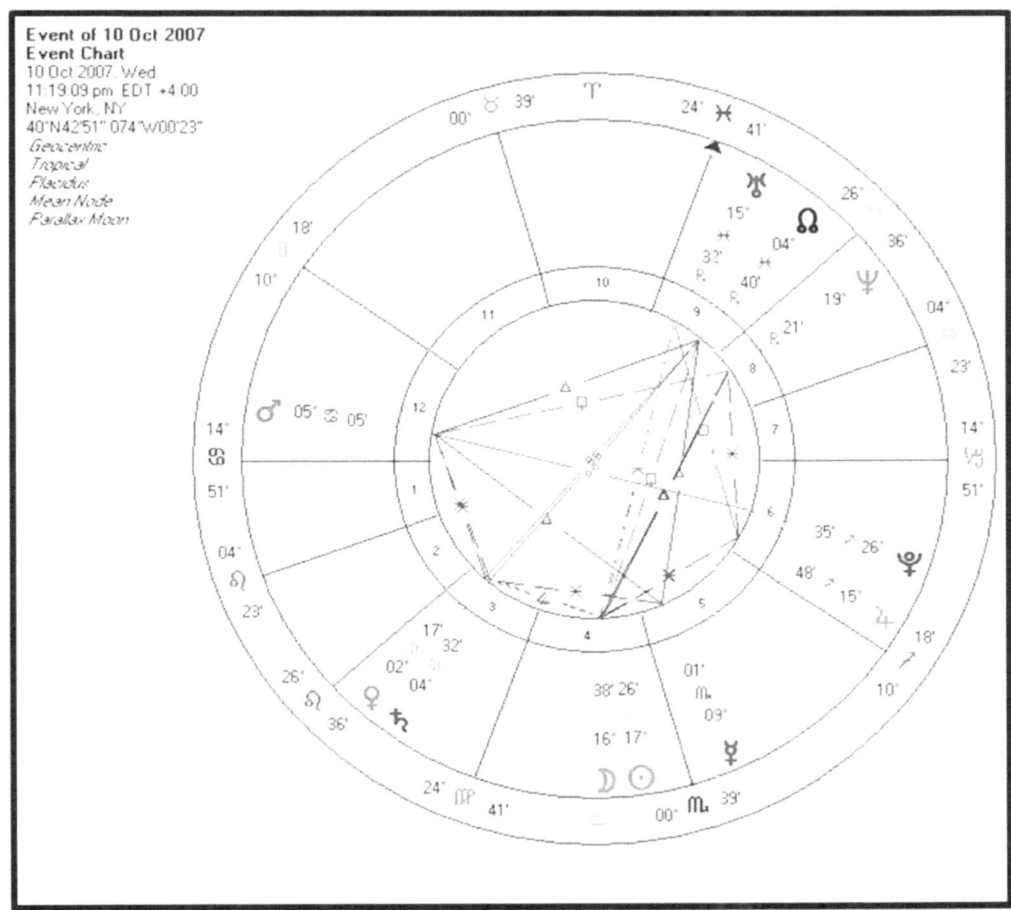

Figure 18 – Planetary Positions October 2007

Step 1: Are there any planets in the 10th House?

There are no planets in the 10th House.

Step 2: Is the New Moon at either the Mid-Heaven (24 Pisces) or the Ascendant (14 Cancer) of the New York Stock Exchange?

The New Moon is not conjunct either of these key locations, but it must be noted that Mars, the aggressive planet, is sitting within orb of making a conjunction to the Ascendant at 14 Cancer. This is an unusual event and warrants caution.

Step 3: Is the New Moon is at an unfavorable aspect to Mars or Neptune?

The New Moon is at a favorable 120 degrees trine to Neptune. Although not properly within orb of being 90 degrees hard aspect to Mars, the New Moon is within 10 degrees of being exactly 90 degrees square to Mars. This warrants some caution.

Step 4: Do any of the outer planets make aspects to Mars or Neptune?

Node is 120 degrees to Mars and Saturn is 60 degrees to Mars.

Step 5: Are Saturn and Uranus at an aspect to one another?

Saturn is just on the verge of coming into orb of being at a 180 degree aspect to Uranus. In the McWhirter methodology, hard aspects between Saturn and Uranus are indicative of trend change.

Step 6: Does the New Moon make any aspects to Jupiter, Saturn, Neptune, Uranus or Pluto?

The New Moon makes a hard 45 degree square to Saturn and a 60 degree aspect to Pluto. Moon makes a 120 degree aspect to Uranus.

Based on the above, we can conclude that Mars was the planetary body to be watched closely.

Analysis: What are the dates when the Moon transits past key planets and key locations?

The daily chart in Figure 19 illustrates the price action of the Dow Jones Average during September-October 2002.

- On Friday, October 12th the Dow Jones pushed higher intra-day, but could not hold the gains. Aggressive Mars was obviously at work. Mercury also weighed weighed into the argument by turning Retrograde. Although it was not immediately known at the time, this was to be the high water mark on the Dow for a good while to come.

- The Moon's transit of Jupiter on the 15th shaved 100 points off the market.

- On the week-end of the 20th-21st, Moon transited past Neptune and the Node. When markets opened on Monday the 22nd, the Moon was passing Uranus and the Mid-Heaven position. This created a trend change and over the next seven sessions, the Dow rallied 160 points.

- On the 31st as Moon transited past Mars, the Dow extended its reach by another 70 points.

- At November 1st, with Mercury turning Direct again, and with Mars drawing closer to the 14 cancer Ascendant point, the Dow shed 160 points.

- On the 7th, Mars again flexed its muscles and the Dow again slumped, shedding 170 points.

This case study illustrates the importance of Mars, especially when Mars is at a key location such as the Ascendant.

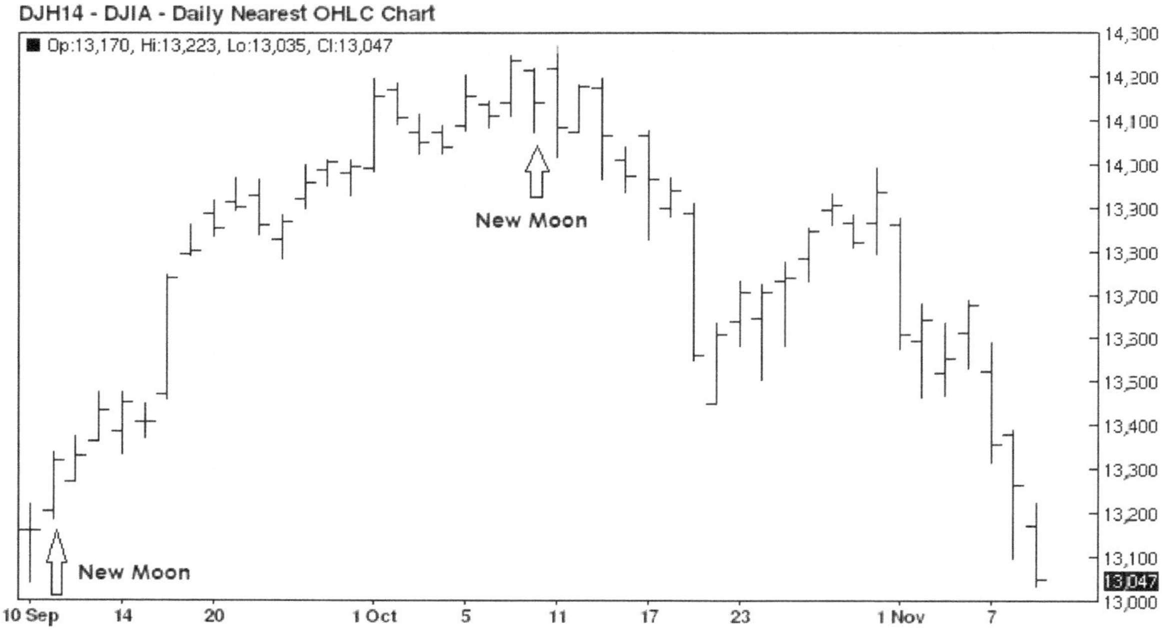

Figure 19 - Daily nearest chart Dow Jones September and October 2007

The Market Low in 2009

In this example, consider the timeframe around February and March, 2009. The New Moon occurred on February 25th.

At the February 25th New Moon, the positions of the planets were:

Sun	7 Pisces
Moon	15 Pisces
North Node	8 Aquarius
Mercury	13 Aquarius
Venus	13 Aries
Mars	16 Aquarius
Jupiter	11 Aquarius
Saturn	19 Virgo
Uranus	21 Pisces
Neptune	24 Aquarius
Pluto	2 Capricorn

Using your software program, generate the horoscope chart for the date of February 25, 2009 using Placidus house divisions. Shift the Placidus house divisions around until the cusp of the first house is at 14 degrees of Cancer.

Your resulting horoscope should look like the zodiac wheel in Figure 20 which has been prepared with Solar Fire Gold.

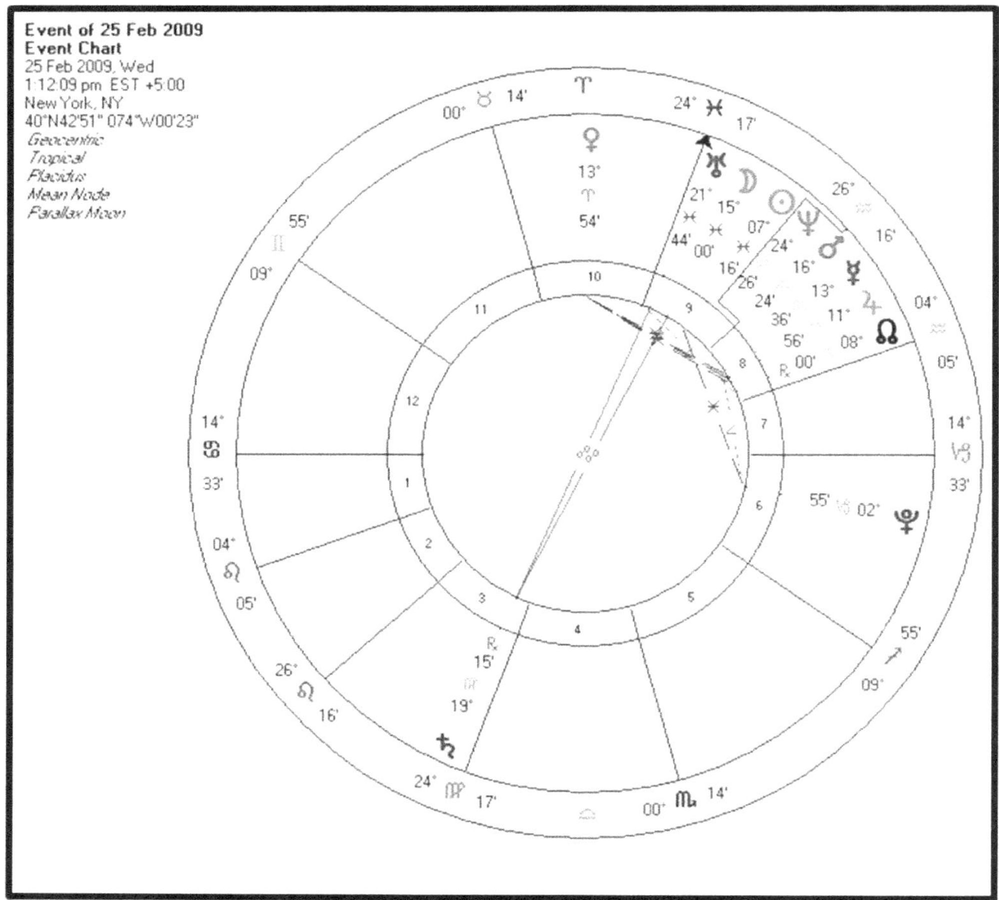

Figure 20 – Planetary Positions February 2009

Step 1: Are there any planets in the 10th House?

Venus in the 10th House. Venus is a friendly planet, so this bodes interesting for the coming lunar cycle.

Step 2: Is the New Moon at the Mid-Heaven (24 Pisces) or the Ascendant (14 Cancer) of the New York Stock Exchange?

New Moon is not at the Mid-Heaven (24 Pisces) position, but is close enough to warrant attention.

Step 3: Is the New Moon at an unfavorable aspect to Mars or Neptune?

The New Moon is not in aspect to Mars or Neptune.

Step 4: Are any of the outer planets in aspect to Mars or Neptune?

Uranus is a benign 30 degrees away from Mars, Neptune is conjunct, Jupiter is conjunct and the Node is conjunct. Definitely a unique set-up that deserves serious attention. Such a grouping of planets within a zodiac sign is called a *stellium.*

Step 5: Are Saturn and Uranus at an aspect to one another?

Saturn is at a 180 degree aspect to Uranus. In the McWhirter methodology, hard aspects between Saturn and Uranus are indicative of trend change.

Step 6: Does the New Moon make any aspects to Jupiter, Saturn, Neptune, Uranus or Pluto?

The New Moon makes a soft 60 degree aspect to Pluto and a soft 30 degree aspect to Jupiter and Node.

Based on the above, we can conclude that the coming lunar cycle will exhibit the makings of trend change.

Analysis: What are the dates when the Moon transits past key planets and key locations?

The daily chart in Figure 21 illustrates the price action of the Dow Jones during February-March 2009.

- On February 26th, Moon passed by the Mid Heaven position and also heavyweight Uranus. The brief few days of consolidation the Dow had been enjoying would abruptly end starting the very next day even as the Moon passed over favorable Venus.

- On the 6th of March, Moon passed by the Ascendant position. The very next trading day was to mark a trend reversal, which we now know from hindsight was the end of the massive sell-off that had started in 2007.

- On the 10th, Moon passed Saturn and the Dow enjoyed a strong up-day. On the 18th, Moon passed Pluto. A brief trend change resulted as the Dow took a couple days to catch its wind again. The 20th marked another trend swing, influenced by the coming passage on the 21st of the Node. On the 22nd, Moon passed Jupiter and on the 23rd Neptune. The 23rd delivered another big up-day for the Dow. The uptrend remained intact with Moon then passing Mars on the 24th and Uranus on the 25th.

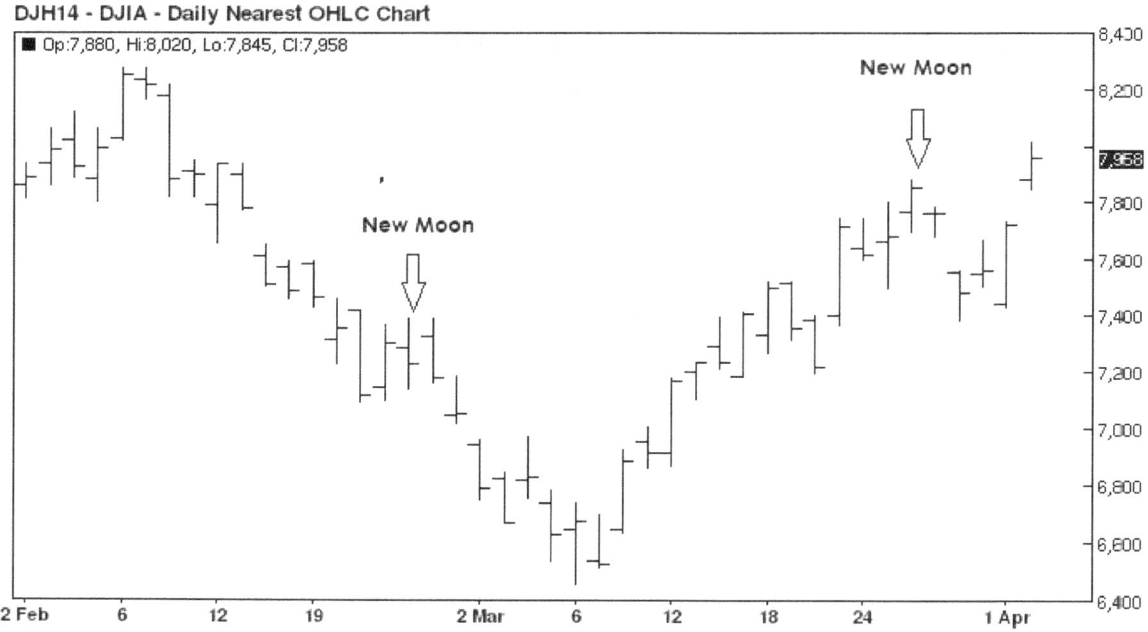

Figure 21-Daily nearest chart Dow Jones February and March 2009

2014 - A Rough Start

2014 will be remembered for the rough and rocky start exhibited by the New York Stock Exchange. The New Moon occurred on January 1st, 2014.

At the January 1 New Moon, the positions of the planets were:

Sun	11 Capricorn
Moon	16 Capricorn
North Node	4 Scorpio
Mercury	13 Capricorn
Venus	26 Capricorn
Mars	12 Libra
Jupiter	15 Cancer
Saturn	20 Scorpio
Uranus	8 Aries
Neptune	3 Pisces
Pluto	11 Capricorn

Using your software program, generate the horoscope chart for the date of January 1, 2014 using Placidus house divisions. Shift the Placidus house divisions around until the cusp of the first house is at 14 degrees of Cancer.

Your resulting horoscope should look like the zodiac wheel in Figure 22 which has been prepared with Solar Fire Gold.

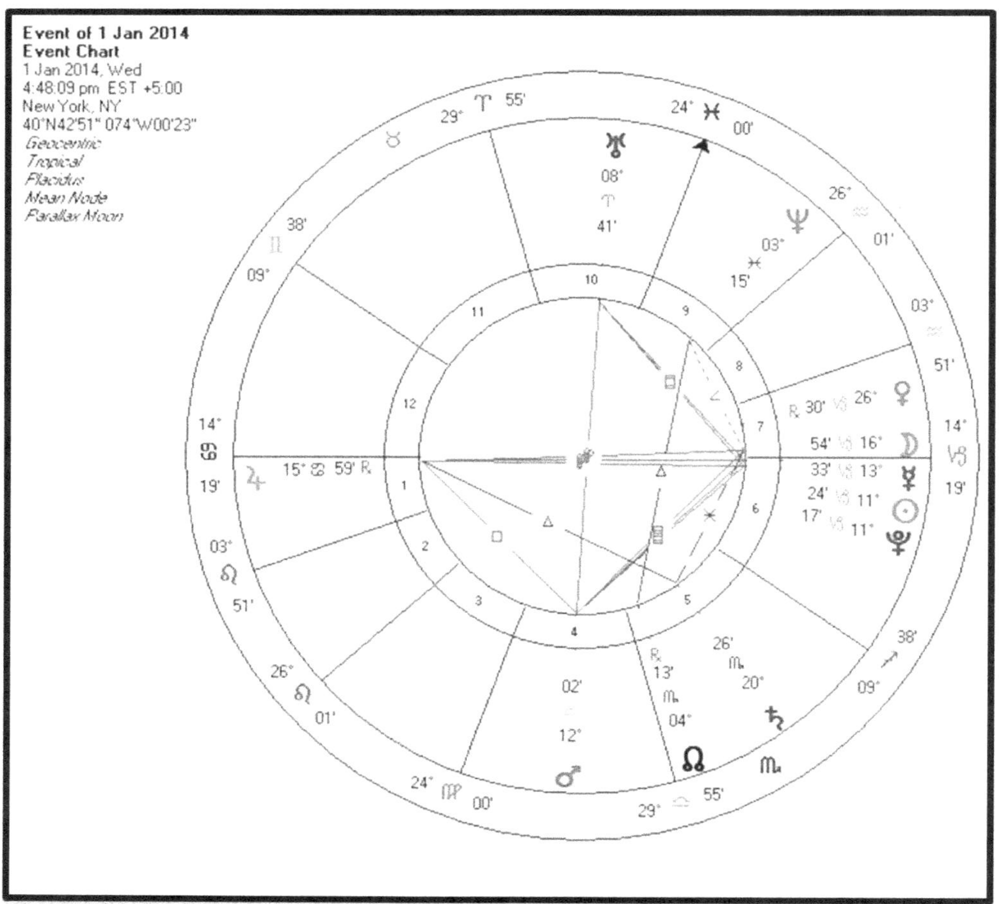

Figure 22 – Planetary Positions January 2014

Step 1: Are there any planets in the 10th House?

Uranus is in the 10th House. Uranus will be a key position to watch during the lunar month.

Step 2: Is the New Moon at the Mid-Heaven (24 Pisces) or the Ascendant (14 Cancer) of the New York Stock Exchange?

New Moon is not at the Mid-Heaven (24 Pisces) position or at the Ascendant position (14 Cancer). But, it is 180 degrees opposite to the Ascendant position which raises a red flag.

Step 3: Is the New Moon at an unfavorable aspect to Mars or Neptune?

The New Moon is at a 90 degree hard aspect to Mars. Caution is warranted.

Step 4: Do any of the outer planets make aspects to Mars or Neptune?

Uranus is a hard 180 degrees opposite from Mars. Jupiter is 90 degrees square. These hard aspects warrant caution.

Step 5: Are Saturn and Uranus at an aspect to one another?

Saturn is not in aspect to Uranus.

Step 6: Does the New Moon make any aspects to Jupiter, Saturn, Neptune, Uranus or Pluto?

The New Moon is 180 degrees opposite Jupiter and 90 degrees hard aspect to Uranus. Both observations suggest that caution is warranted.

Analysis: What are the dates when the Moon transits past key planets and key locations?

The following daily chart in Figure 23 illustrates the price action of the Dow Jones during January 2014.

- Even though the analysis of the New Moon suggested that caution should be in order, there was nothing to indicate whether any one of the hard aspects would be more important than another. As January drew near, what we did know was that the Dow was sitting at a 1.272 Fibonacci extension of the 2007 to 2009 decline. This critical level put in place the argument that the market was ripe for a pullback. However, the possibility also existed that the market would press higher in a volatile fashion to perhaps test a 1.414 extension or even a 1.618 extension. This observation raises a key point, that being the McWhirter method should be used where possible in conjunction with other esoteric mathematical techniques such as Fibonacci retracements. On January 2, 2014 the market recorded a down day which suggested a possible trend change. An alert trader seeing this would have hopefully placed a stop loss somewhere underneath the low of the day.

- Price action firmed up as Moon passed the Mid Heaven location on the 5th and Uranus on the 6th.

- On the 13th, price dropped sharply quite likely triggering numerous stop loss orders in the process.

- For those still in the market, on the 14th with Moon approaching the Ascendant and Jupiter, price attempted a rally. This rally, however, was unable to surpass the highs recorded at the start of January – another warning sign.

- On the 22nd Moon transited aggressive Mars. The very next day, price action on the Dow gapped down and broke some key moving averages.

- On the 28th, as Moon transited Pluto and Venus, markets calmed themselves on news that Turkey and India were raising interest rates to prop up their currencies.

- On the 29th with these transits complete, markets fell again as the Fed tapered its bond buying by another $10 billion per month.

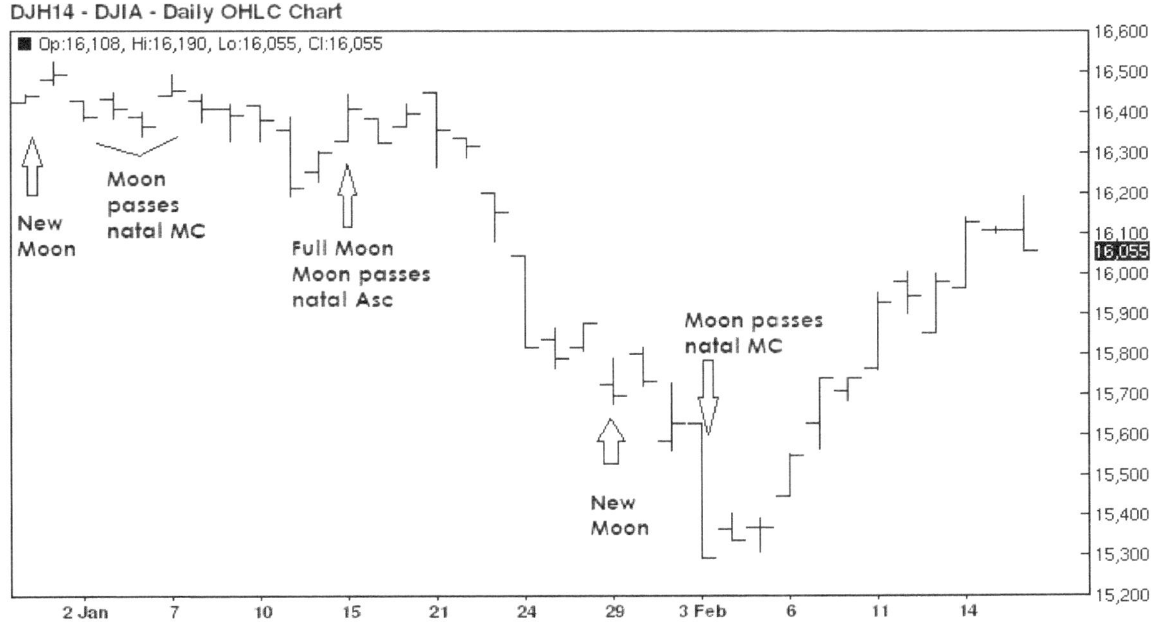

Figure 23 – Daily chart Dow Jones January 2014

10. IDENTIFYING TREND CHANGES ON INDIVIDUAL STOCKS

The McWhirter approach to the stock market further includes using astrology to predict trend changes on individual stocks or commodity futures.

This approach is based on transiting Sun and the major planets making aspects to the natal Sun, the natal Moon and the sign ruler positions as determined from the first trade chart. This approach also focuses on aspects of transiting Sun and other planets to natal Mars and Jupiter. All in all quite a complex approach. Therefore, when using the McWhirter method to study individual stocks or commodity futures, I simplify matters by being alert to those times when the following events happen:

- Sun makes 0, 90, 120, 180 degree aspects to natal Sun

- Mars makes 0, 90, 120, 180 degree aspects to natal Sun

- Mars makes 0, 90, 120, 180 degree aspects to natal Mars

- Mars makes 0, 90, 120, 180 degree aspects to natal Jupiter

- Sun and/or Mars make 0, 90, 120, or 180 degree aspects to the "ruler" of the Sun sign

- Transiting Saturn makes 0 and 90 degree aspects to natal Sun

- Transiting Jupiter makes 0 and 90 degree aspects to natal Sun

These events are not necessarily frequent. Earth takes 365 days to orbit the Sun. Therefore, from our vantage point here on Earth we will see Sun making 0, 90, 120 and 130 degree aspects to natal Sun only four times a year.

Mars takes 687 days to orbit the Sun. From our vantage point here on Earth we will see Mars make various aspects to natal Sun, natal Mars and natal Jupiter only a handful of times each year.

Saturn takes 29.42 years to orbit the Sun and Jupiter 11.85 years. From our vantage point here on Earth, Saturn and Jupiter will make aspects to the natal Sun very infrequently. But, when these aspects do occur, they can be powerful events.

Not every stock or commodity will exhibit alignments to all of these various aspects. When examining a stock or commodity future, it is advised to look back in time several years to see which aspects most often repeat themselves. This will then give you a valid model to follow going forward in time.

11. Setting Up the First Trade Chart

The starting point for using the McWhirter approach to identify trend changes on individual stocks is the *first trade chart*. The First Trade chart is a zodiac wheel that shows the position of the planets on the day the stock (or commodity future) in question first officially started trading on a financial exchange.

Does the McWhirter technique works for all stocks? The answer is a definite no. In order for astrology to be applied to an individual stock, that stock must be seen to be trading decent volumes every day. Stocks that have days where trading volume is low or negligible are not suitable candidates for the McWhirter method because not enough people and therefore not enough emotional energy are impacting price movement. This then rules out many of the micro-cap stocks that trade on the OTC market in the USA or on the TSX Venture Exchange in Canada. This also rules out stocks having low trading volumes because large blocks of stock are owned by passive investors who choose not to trade.

The first step in setting up a first trade chart is to determine the date when the stock first started trading. The site www.investingsuccess.ca has links to data tables that provide many first trade dates. If there is a stock for which you absolutely cannot identify the first trade date, a phone call to the Exchange in question can often yield good results. I have had friendly, favorable responses when seeking information from the Toronto Stock Exchange, the London Stock exchange and the Australian Stock Exchange. Evidently I am not the only person using astrology to have contacted these exchanges.

The second step is to determine the positions of the planets on the First Trade date. As noted previously in this publication, the best way to obtain this data is with a software program such as Solar Fire Gold. It is also possible to use the McWhirter method by manually preparing a horoscope chart showing planetary placements. To help you in this undertaking, you can make photocopies of the blank zodiac wheel contained in the Appendix to this Study Guide.

If not using a software program to determine planetary placements, planetary positions can be found in a Geocentric Ephemeris such as *The New American Ephemeris for the 21st Century*, authored by Enrique Pottenger.

It is also possible to find Ephemeris tables on line. One reliable website is http://www.astro.com.

When identifying trend changes on individual stocks, the McWhirter approach requires the Sun to be placed on the cusp of the first House. If using a program such as Solar Fire Gold, in the chart basic set-up options instruct the program to draw the First Trade date chart so that Sun is at the cusp of the first House. If preparing a chart manually using the blank zodiac wheel provided in the Appendix, position the Sun at the cusp of the first house, and then proceed to mark off the remainder of the houses in 30 degree increments. Place the planets at the proper locations using data from the Ephemeris tables. Determine if any planets make aspects to Sun, Moon or Jupiter. (Sun represents the very essence of a company. According to McWhirter- the Moon refers to the attitude of the public towards the company and Jupiter being an expansive, positive planet governs the fortunes of the company). The rules concerning degree separations for aspects that were discussed previously still apply. That is,

McWhirter Rules for Aspect Angles

- In the case of a 0 degree conjunction 180 degree opposition, it is acceptable to have planets within 10 degrees of being opposite to each other.

- In the case of a 90 degree square, it is acceptable to have planets within 5 degrees of being square to each other.

- In the case of a 60 degree sextile aspect, it is acceptable to have planets within 5 degrees of being sextile to each other.

- In the case of a 30 degree semi-sextile aspect, it is acceptable to have planets within 3 degrees of being semi-sextile to each other.

- In the case of a 120 degree trine aspect, it is acceptable to have planets within 5 degrees of being trine to each other

Next, determine the ruler of the sign that the Sun is in.

The concept of ruler-ship is an old one and goes back many hundreds of years in the annals of astrology. The following is a summary of planetary ruler-ships.

Zodiac Sign	Ruling Planet
Aries	Mars
Taurus and Libra	Venus
Gemini and Virgo	Mercury
Cancer	Moon
Leo	Sun
Sagittarius	Jupiter
Aquarius and Capricorn	Saturn (Uranus)
Scorpio	Mars (Pluto)
Pisces	Neptune

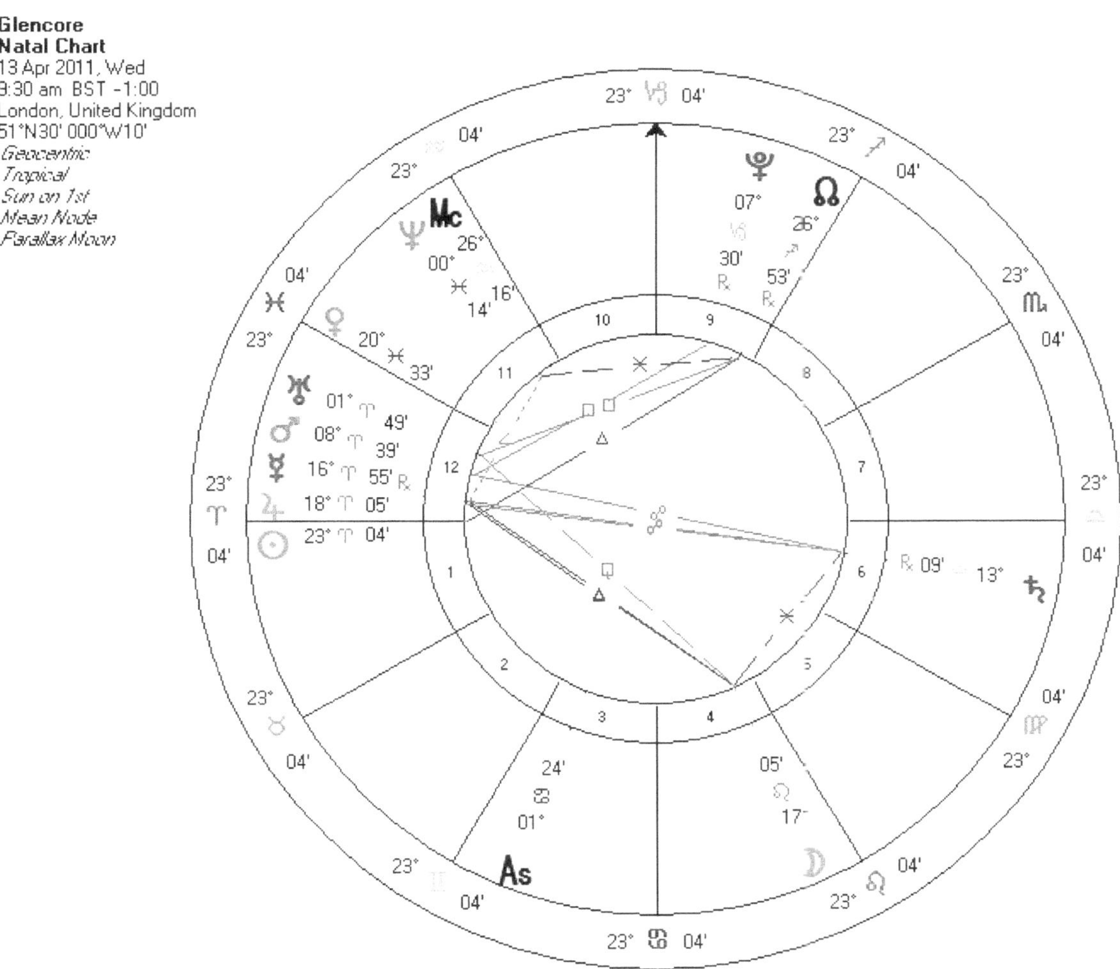

Exercise #2 - Glencore

Glencore is a global commodity trading firm with interests ranging from mining to oil and gas to agriculture. Glencore first started trading on the London Stock Exchange on April 13, 2011.

1. What is the sign and degree position of Jupiter?
2. Does the Sun make an aspect angle to Jupiter?
3. What is the aspect relation between Jupiter and Saturn?
4. What is the sign and degree position of Moon?

Please refer to the De-Brief section of this book for answers

12. FIRST TRADE CHART CASE STUDIES

ANZ Banking Group Limited (Australia: ANZ)

Australia and New Zealand Banking Group Limited, through its subsidiaries, provides various banking and financial products and services to retail, small business, corporate, and institutional customers in Australia, New Zealand, the Asia Pacific region, the Middle East, Europe, and the United States. ANZ started trading publicly on July 31, 1969.

The First Trade chart in Figure 24 has been prepared with Solar Fire Gold and illustrates the position of the various planets at 31 July, 1969. Sun has been placed on the cusp of the first House.

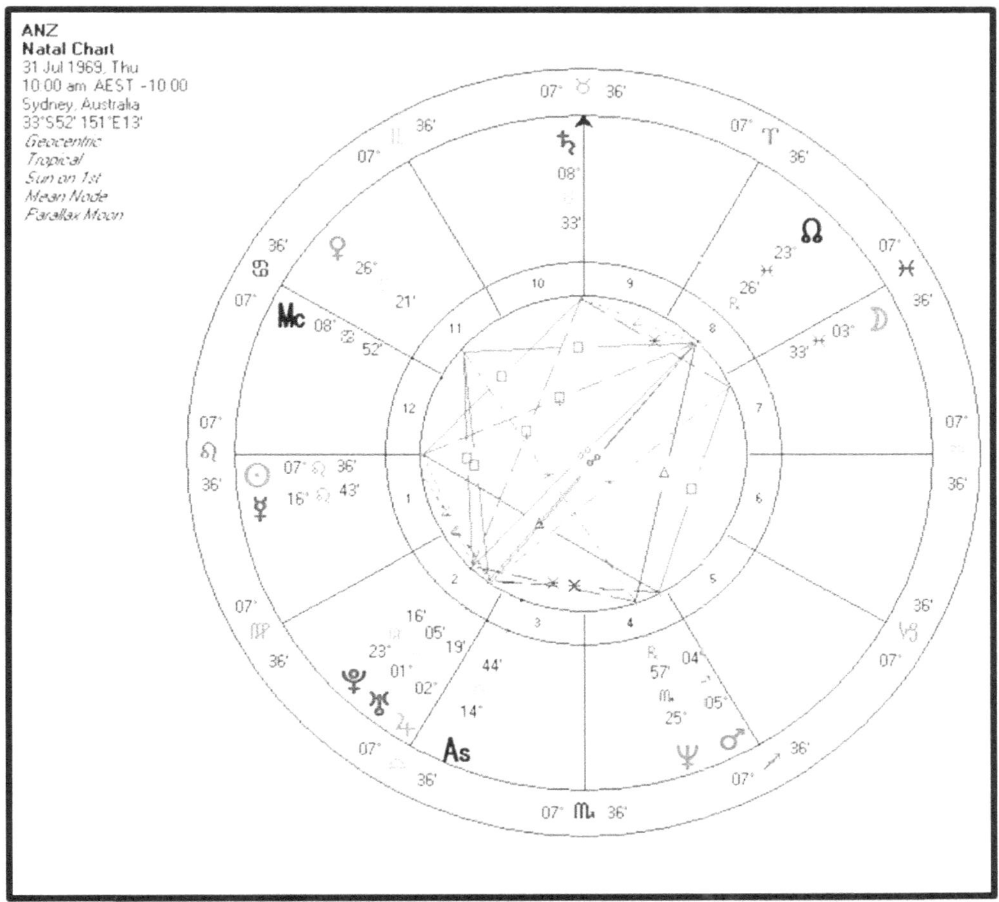

Figure 24 – ASX: ANZ First Trade chart

Step 1: What aspects are present to Sun, Moon and Jupiter?

Sun can be seen making a hard 90 degree square aspect to Saturn. Sun also makes a 120 degree aspect to Mars. Moon is at a favorable 60 degrees to Saturn, but an unfavorable hard 90 degrees to Mars. Jupiter is a favorable 60 degrees to Mars, a favorable 60 degrees to Sun but a hard 90 degrees square to Venus. More importantly, Jupiter is at 0 degrees to heavy-weight Uranus.

These many complicated aspects suggest a stock that will <u>not</u> enjoy smooth sailing at all times. The monthly price chart in Figure 25 illustrates this point exactly. The share price rose from 2000 to 2007, but then gave it all back by late 2008. Since then, share price has risen again. This has certainly been a painful journey for long term shareholders. If you are a long term shareholder that prefers to buy and hold, it is not wise to invest in a stock having many complicated aspects in its First Trade chart.

Figure 25 – Monthly price chart, ANZ

Step 2: What sign is Sun in and what is the ruler of that sign?

Sun is in Leo and Sun also happens to be the ruler of Leo. Hence, transiting Sun making aspects to the natal Sun position at 7 degrees of Leo will be important to watch for as trend changes may occur at these aspects.

Step 3: When will transiting Jupiter or Saturn aspect the natal Sun position?

Times when Saturn or Jupiter make 0, 90 or 180 degree hard aspects to natal Sun should be watched carefully. Saturn takes nearly 30 years to make one full cycle around the twelve signs of the zodiac and Jupiter takes just under 12 years. Therefore, these aspects to the natal Sun will <u>not</u> be frequent. When they do occur, they can take a while to fully complete themselves. As they complete themselves, expect to see above normal price volatility.

To illustrate, note the weekly chart in Figure 26. From October 2012 to November 2013, transiting Saturn slowly made its 90 degree aspect to natal Sun. This time frame even included a Saturn retrograde event. Notice the price volatility on the weekly chart that an aggressive trader could have taken advantage of by using moving averages and other technical indicators. Notice also that shortly after this transit completed itself, there was yet another change in trend with momentum turning down and price falling from the $34 level to the $29 level. Such is the powerful influence that Saturn can exert. The next hard aspect of Saturn to natal Sun will not occur for several more years.

On this same chart, notice the timeframe when transiting Jupiter slowly made its 90 degree hard aspect to natal Sun. Shortly after this aspect started forming, price hit a significant low at just under $18 and then started trending higher. An alert trader watching Jupiter's progress at this time would also have been watching moving averages and other indicators for evidence of trend changes.

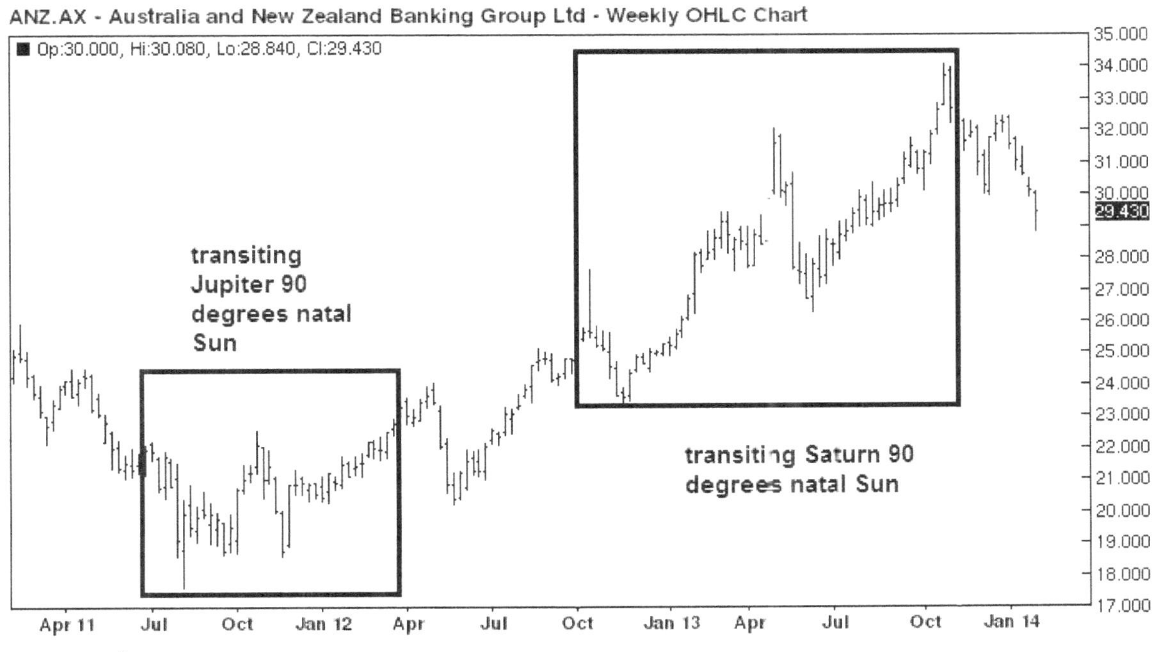

Figure 26-Weekly price chart, ANZ

Step 4: When will transiting Sun or Mars make aspects to natal Sun and natal Mars locations?

During the time frame from late 2012 through 2013 the following events transpired:

2012-2013 Dates	Astrological Occurrence	Occurrence Number
November 20 through December 4, 2012	Transiting Sun 120 degrees natal Sun. Sun 0 degrees natal Mars.	1
January 1 through January 14, 2013	Transiting Mars 180 degrees natal Sun	2
January 18 through February 5, 2013	Transiting Sun 180 degrees natal Sun	3
March 13 through March 31, 2013	Transiting Sun 120 degrees natal Sun, Mars 120 degrees natal Sun	4
April 18 through May 7, 2013	Transiting Sun 90 degrees natal Sun. Mars 90 degrees Sun also.	5
June 7 through June 13, 2013	Mars 180 degrees natal Mars, Mars 90 degrees natal Moon	6
July 21 through August 9, 2013	Transiting Sun 0 degrees natal Sun	7
August 25 through September 23, 2013	Transiting Mars 0 degrees natal Sun	8
October 22 through November 9, 2013	Transiting Sun 90 degrees natal Sun	9

The daily chart in Figure 27 illustrates these 9 different events. Not all of these events delivered trend changes worthy of headline news. But, to the trader or short term investor following the progress of transiting Sun and Mars while using technical indicators, there were certainly several opportunities to benefit from. As noted previously in this publication, the use of Fibonacci retracements and extensions is also important when trying to identify trend changes. For example, in Figure 27 astrological occurrence number 6 aligns nicely to a 0.618 retracement of the up-move that started at occurrence number 1 and ended at occurrence 5. The price highs made during astrological occurrence number 9 align fairly well to a 1.272 extension of the down-move from May through June 2013.

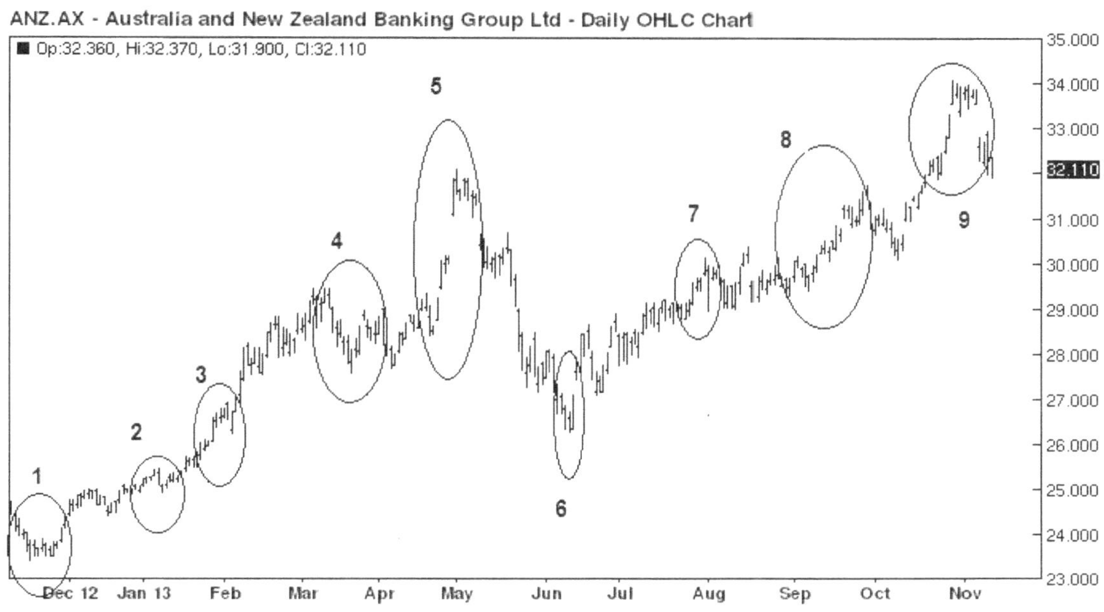

Figure 27 – Daily price chart, ANZ

Step 5: Are there aspects involving the "ruler" of the Sun sign? What about aspects to natal Jupiter?

In step 2 above, we have established that Sun is the ruler of Leo, the sign that Sun appears in on the First Trade chart. We have just studied aspects to natal Sun in step 4. During the timespan depicted in Figure 27, there were no aspects to natal Jupiter.

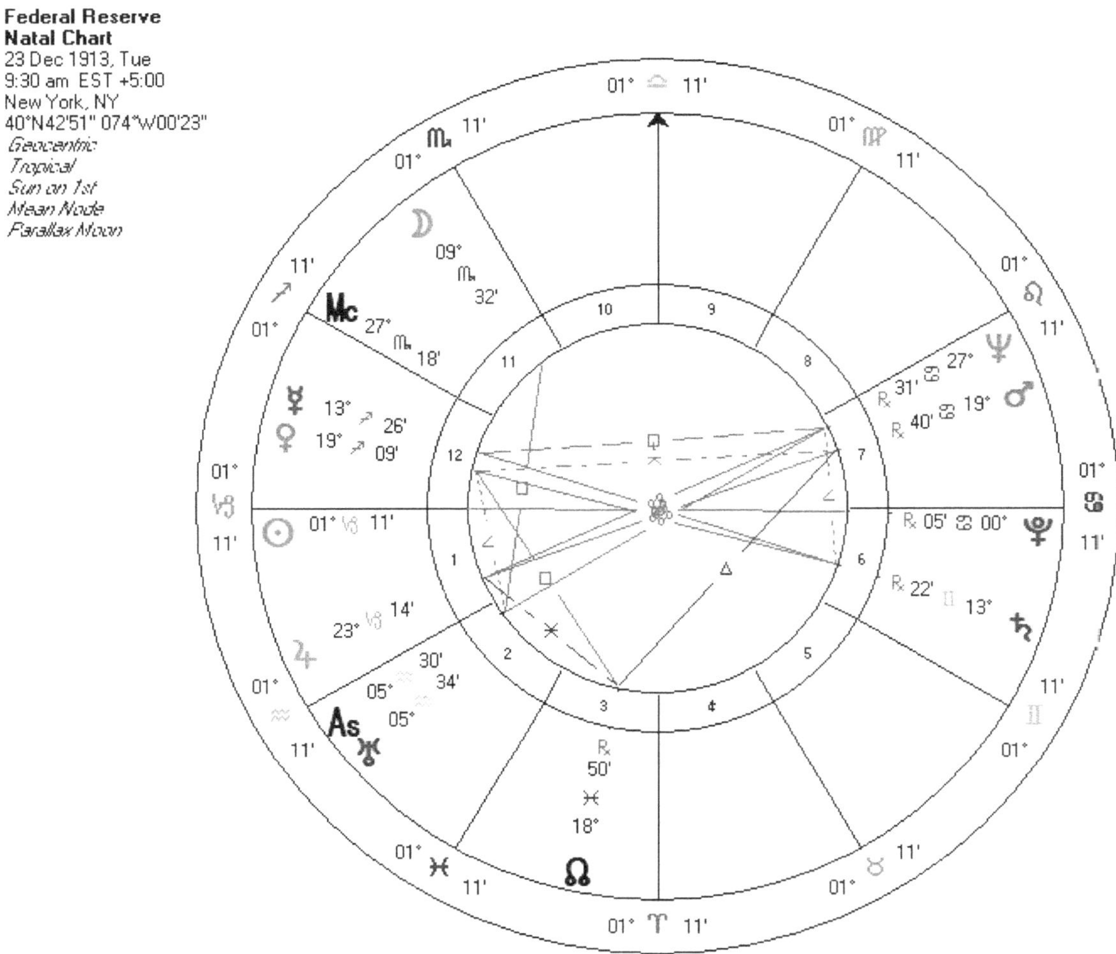

Exercise #3 – US Federal Reserve

The horoscope in this exercise is that of the US Federal Reserve, which was born in December 1913.

1. What sign is Sun located in?
2. What is the ruler of this sign?
3. To which planet does Sun make a 180 degree aspect?
4. To which planets does Jupiter make aspects to? Describe these aspects.
5. To what planet does Moon make an aspect to? Describe this aspect.
6. When will Saturn again transit past natal Sun?

Please refer to the De-Brief section of this book for answers.

Blackberry (Toronto Stock Exchange: BB)

Want to generate some laughter at the next social event you go to? Just reach in your pocket and pull out your Blackberry smart phone. From 2011 to 2014, Canadian smart phone maker Blackberry went from *'hero to zero'*. But, despite the obituaries crafted by many analysts, the company still refuses to die. Blackberry (formerly called Research in Motion) started trading publicly on October 21, 1997.

The First Trade chart in Figure 28 has been prepared with Solar Fire Gold and illustrates the position of the various planets at October 21, 1997. Sun has been placed on the cusp of the first House.

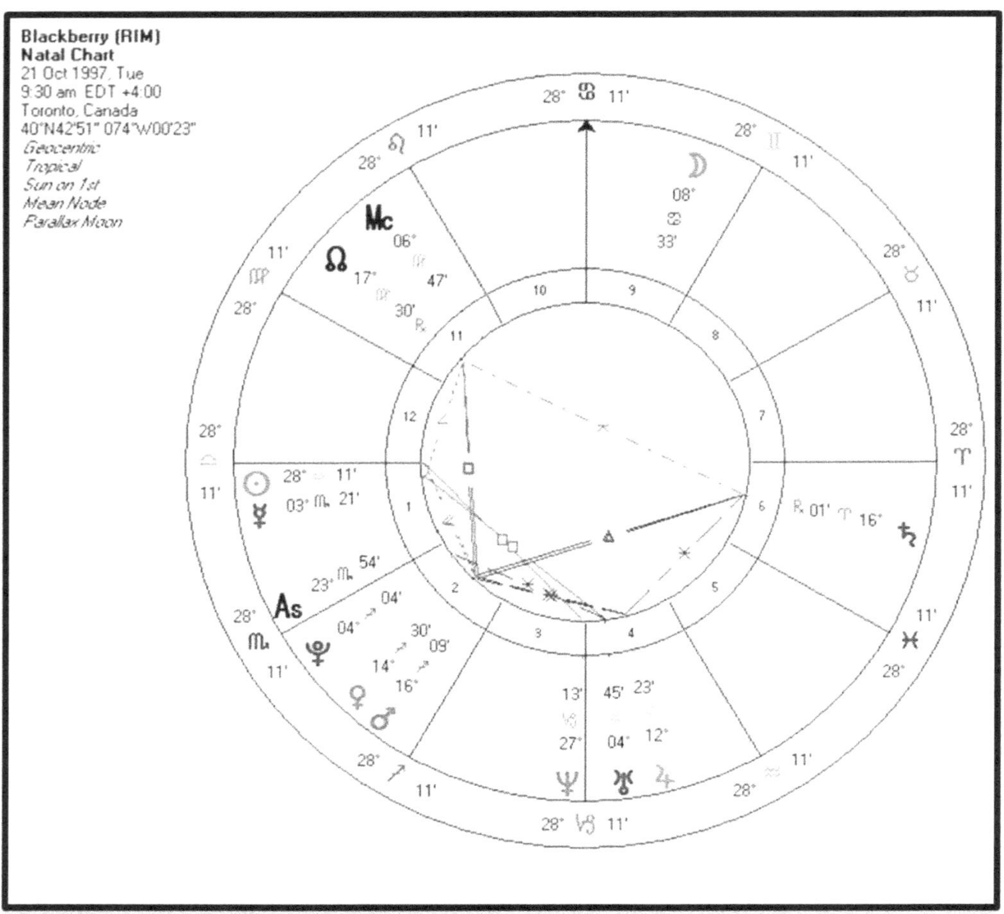

Figure 28 – Blackberry First Trade chart

Step 1: Are any aspects are present to Sun, Moon and Jupiter?

Sun is 90 degrees square to both Uranus and Neptune. To modern astrologers, Uranus is the planet of technology, communications and broadcasting while Neptune is regarded as a planet that governs electricity and electrical devices. Rather appropriate for a smart phone maker don't you think? There are no aspects to Moon. Jupiter is a favorable 60 degrees to Saturn and a favorable 60 degrees to Mars and Venus. From this we can deduce that this company may encounter some issues as a result of the hard aspects to Uranus and Neptune. But, with no unfavorable hard aspects to Moon and Jupiter, this is a company that should survive for many years to come – and as just noted it continues to survive despite the many repeated predictions of its death.

Step 2: What sign is Sun in and what is the ruler of that sign?

Sun is in Libra and Venus is the "ruler" of Libra.

Step 3: When will transiting Jupiter or Saturn aspect the natal Sun position?

From January 2011 to November 2012, slow moving Saturn eased past the natal Sun location. The weekly chart in Figure 29 shows the devastation that accrued. An alert trader seeing the weekly chart technical indicators announce a change of trend would have likely exited his or her position before Saturn wreaked too much havoc.

From mid-June 2014 to mid-August 2014, transiting Jupiter made its 90 degree aspect to natal Sun. Blackberry dismissed its CEO late in 2013. The new CEO is suggesting a return to positive cash flow in 2015. This Jupiter 90 degree aspect to natural Sun evidently sparked some positive shareholder emotion and share price during this transit surged from C$8.50 to $12.50.

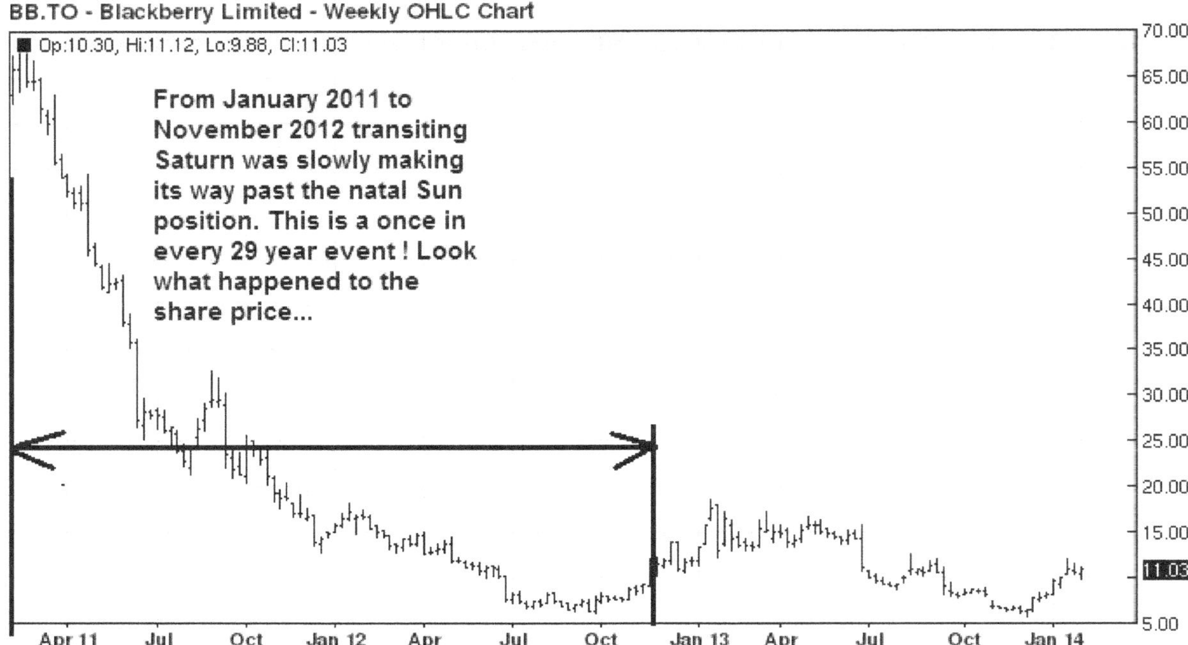

Figure 29 – Blackberry and the Saturn transit

Step 4: When will transiting Sun or Mars make aspects to natal Sun and natal Mars locations?

There were several aspects to natal Sun and natal Mars from late 2012 to early 2014 as outlined in the following table.

2012-2014 Dates	Astrological Occurrence	Occurrence Number
October 15 through October 30, 2012	Transiting Sun 0 degrees natal Sun.	1
October 18 through November 9, 2012	Transiting Mars 0 degrees natal Mars	2
November 30 through December 15, 2012	Transiting Sun 0 degrees natal Mars	3
December 13 through January 29, 2013	Transiting Mars 90 degrees natal Sun, Sun 90 degrees natal Sun	4
April 6 through May 1, 2013	Transiting Sun 180 degrees natal Sun. Mars 180 degrees Sun also.	5
July 12 through August 1, 2013	Transiting Sun 90 degrees natal Sun	7
August 12 through September 9, 2013	Transiting Mars 90 degrees natal Sun	8
October 13 through October 31, 2013	Transiting Sun 0 degrees natal Sun	9
January 9 to January 28, 2014	Transiting Sun 0 degrees natal Sun	10
January 21 to April 13, 2014	Transiting Mars 0 degrees natal Sun	
July 3 to August 9, 2014	Transiting Mars 0 degrees natal Sun. Sun is 90 degrees natal Sun. Jupiter is 90 degrees natal Sun.	

Figure 30 illustrates occurrences 1 through 4. During each of these occurrences, notice that price suddenly surged above a sideways consolidation level to create a definite trend change. An alert trader knowing that these occurrences were in effect would have been watching chart technical indicators for some evidence of trend change.

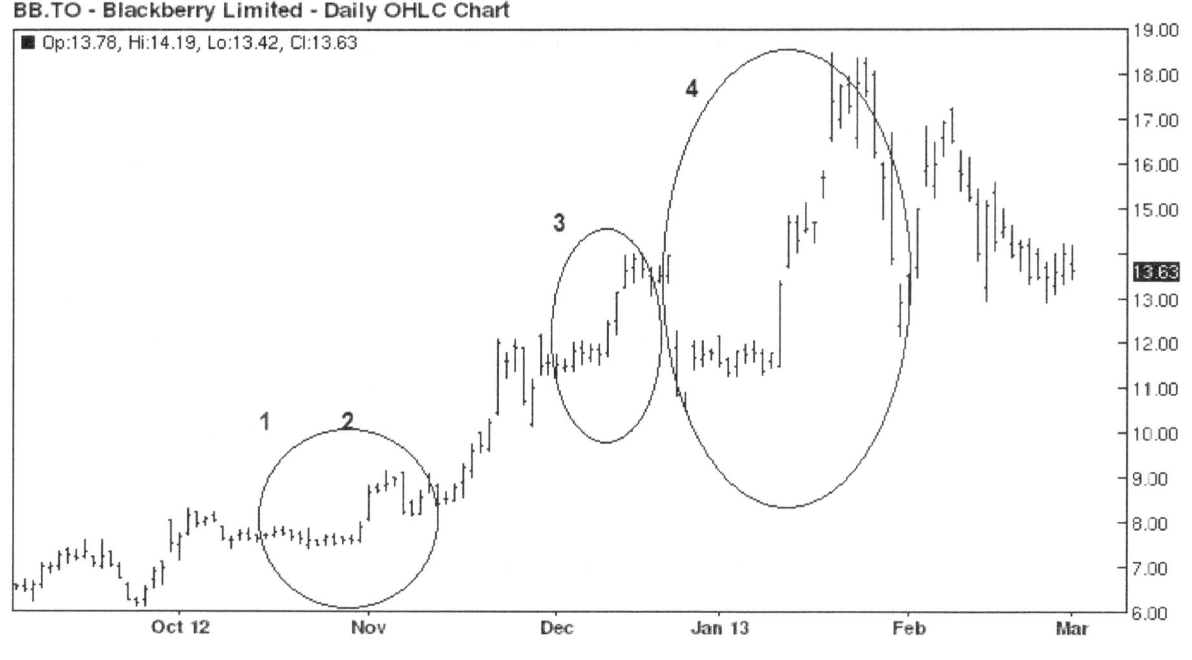

Figure 30 – Blackberry Sun and Mars transits

Step 5: What about aspects involving the "ruler" of the Sun sign? What about aspects to natal Jupiter? What about aspects to natal Moon?

From June 23 through July 8, transiting Sun passed by the natal Moon position. In Figure 31, this event is denoted as occurrence number 6. Notice the hard drop in share price as this transit unfolded. Figure 31 also illustrates occurrences 5 through 10 from the above Table.

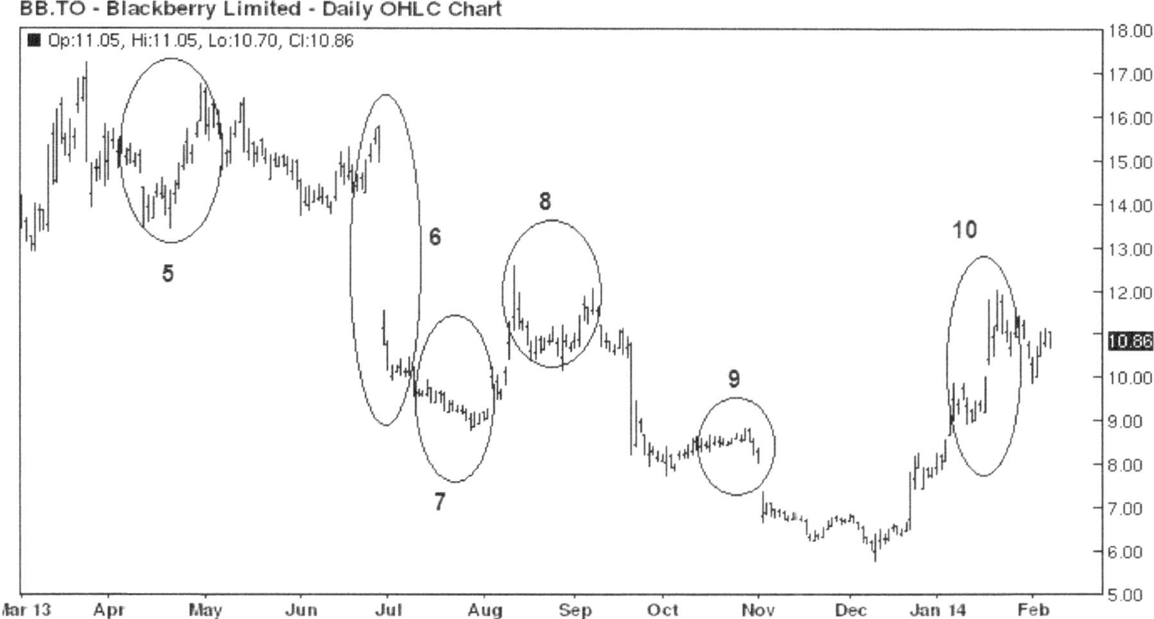

Figure 31 – additional Blackberry Sun and Mars transits

We noted in step 2 that Venus was the "ruler" of the Sun's sign Libra. In the chart in Figure 30, note that transiting Venus made an aspect to natal Sun in November 2012. Contributed to the rise in share price from around $9 to the $12 area. In late December 2012, transiting Venus made a 0 degree aspect to natal Venus and natal Mars. Note how share price dropped from the $14 level to just under $11 as this transit stirred up emotion amongst traders and investors.

From October 12 to October 29, 2013 transiting Venus again made a 0 degree aspect to natal Venus. In Figure 31, note the hard drop in price as this transit completed itself. t is always interesting to observe overlapping events. This Venus transit occurred at the same time as occurrence 9 which had transiting Sun passing 0 degrees natal Sun.

In mid-January 2013, aggressive Mars passed by natal Jupiter and spa ked a powerful rally that took share price up to $18. This rally can be seen in Figure 32. But, as Mars completed this transit, note that share price fell right back down again to the $12 area, no doubt catching many traders unaware.

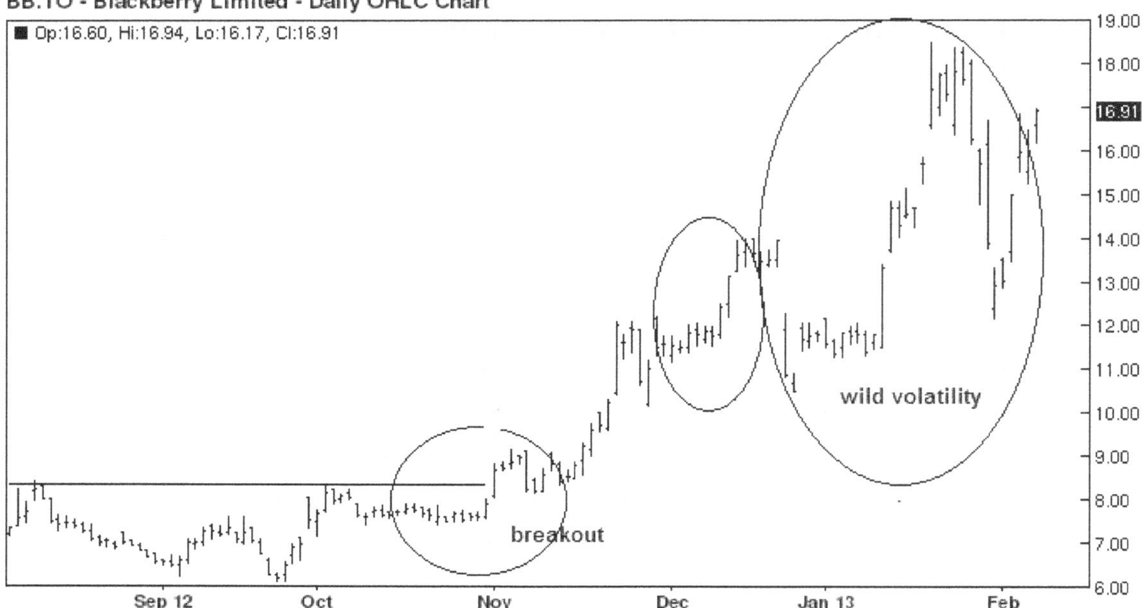

Figure 32 – Blackberry transits involving Venus and Jupiter

Figure 33 illustrates what happened during 2013 as Sun passed natal Jupiter. Notice the violent whipsaw action that no doubt caught many by surprise. In late June through late August all of Sun, Jupiter and Mars moved past the natal Moon location. This overwhelmed emotions and share price took a severe beating. Note also that this price drop corresponds to Sun transiting past the natal Moon location. This reinforces a valuable point. One must be particularly alert for increased price volatility when multiple astrological events are seen to overlap one another.

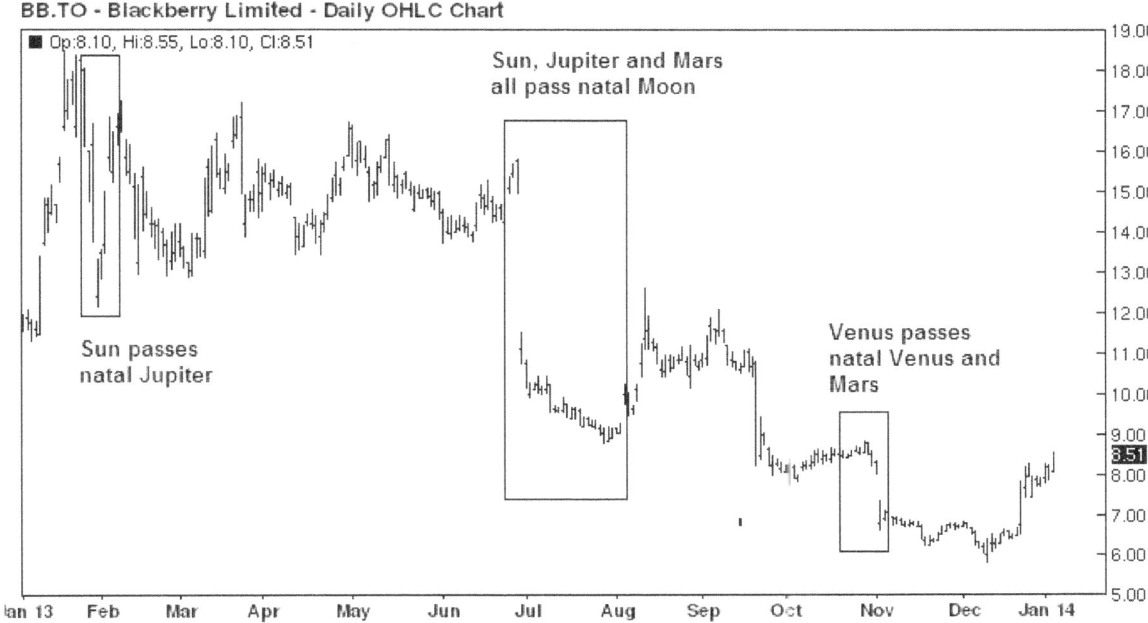

Figure 33 – Blackberry 2013 transits

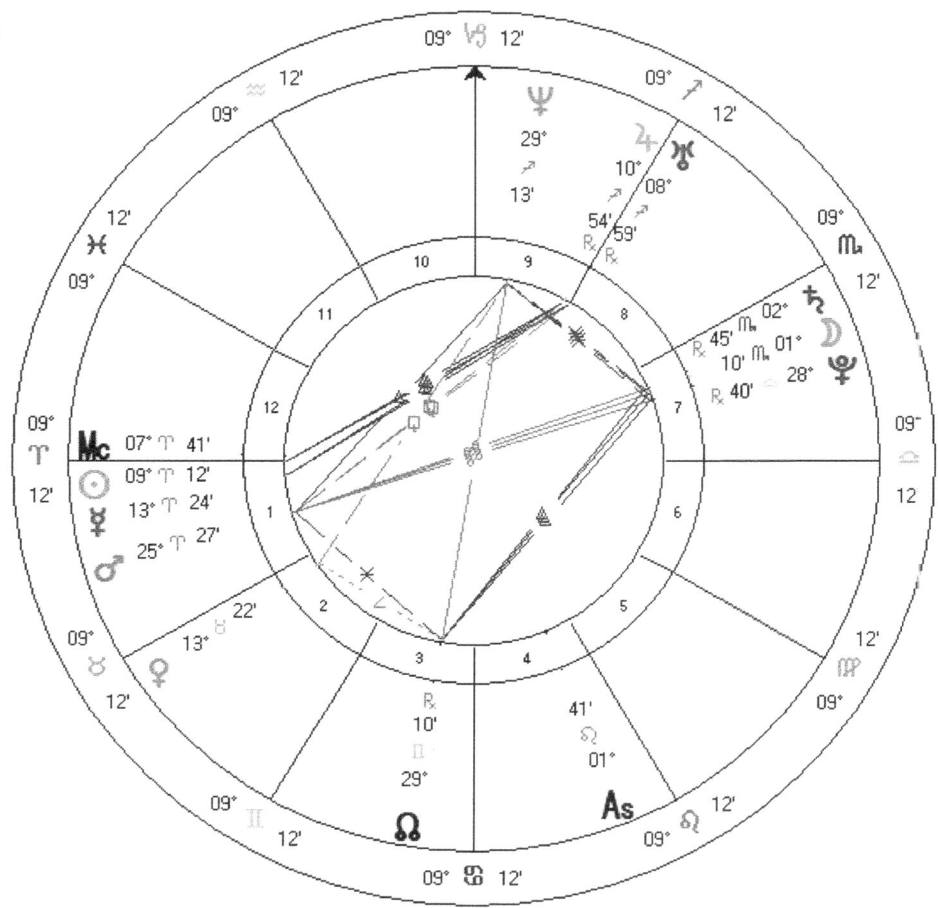

Exercise #4 – Crude Oil futures

Crude Oil futures started trading in New York on March 30, 1983. The horoscope in this exercise shows planetary placements at that first trade date.

1. In what sign does the Mid-Heaven (MC) appear?
2. What is the ruler of that sign?
3. What celestial bodies are conjunct to the MC?
4. A rectangular shape can be seen in this horoscope wheel. Which celestial bodies make up this rectangular shape?

Please refer to the De-Brief section of this book for answers.

CN RAIL (Toronto Stock Exchange: CNR)

Canadian National Railway Company (CNR) is engaged in the rail and related transportation business. CNR's network of approximately 20,100 route miles spans Canada and mid-America, connecting three coasts: the Atlantic, the Pacific and the Gulf of Mexico, serving the ports of Vancouver, Prince Rupert (British Columbia), Montreal, Halifax, New Orleans, and Mobile (Alabama) and metropolitan areas of Toronto, Buffalo, Chicago, Detroit, Duluth (Minnesota)/Superior (Wisconsin), Green Bay (Wisconsin), Minneapolis/St. Paul, Memphis and Jackson (Mississippi), with connections to all points in North America. CN started trading publicly on November 17, 1995.

The First Trade chart in Figure 34 has been prepared with Solar Fire Gold and illustrates the position of the various planets at November 17, 1995. Sun has been placed on the cusp of the first House.

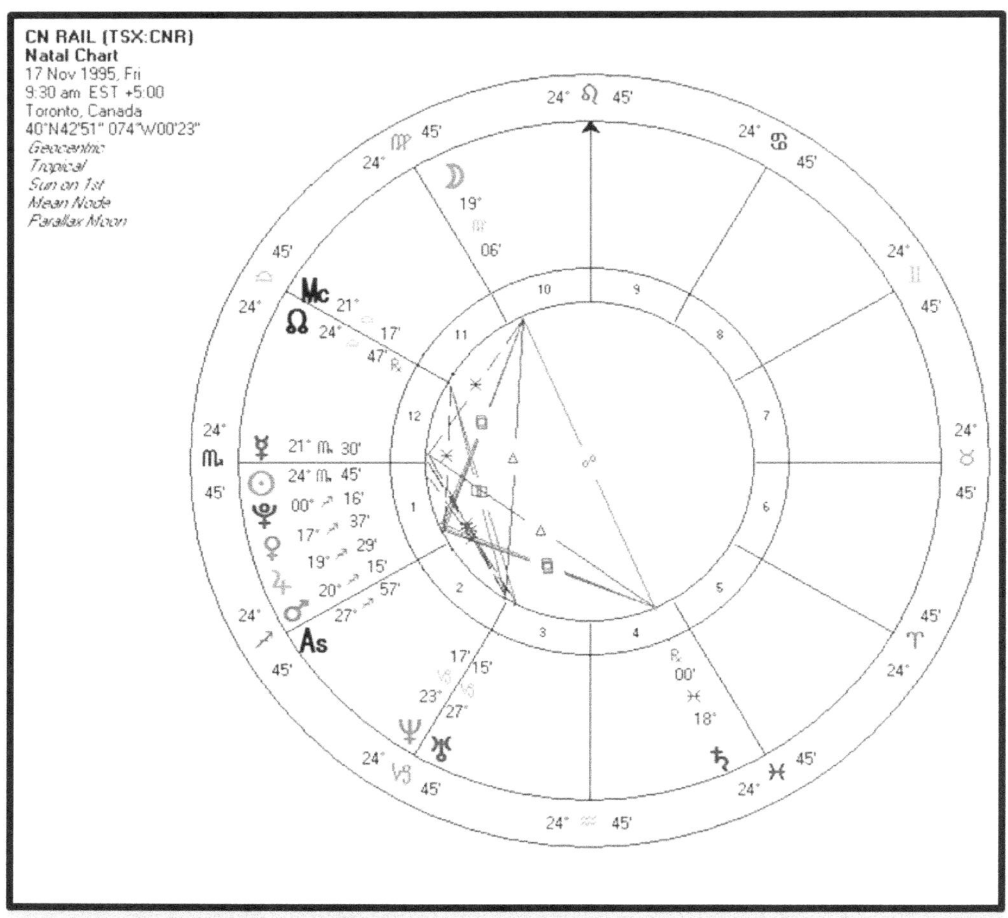

Figure 34 - CN Rail First Trade chart

Step 1: What aspects are present to Sun, Moon and Jupiter?

Sun is a positive 60 degrees to Uranus and Neptune. Sun is a benign 30 degrees to Mars and a favorable 120 degrees to Saturn. Moon is 180 degrees to repressive Saturn. Moon generally represents the public so from this aspect one can infer that there *may* be times when the public experiences significantly dampened changes of opinion towards the company. Jupiter is 0 degrees to Mars which implies that some volatility can be expected. Jupiter is a hard 90 degrees to Moon which also implies that some volatility can be expected.

Step 2: What sign is Sun in and what is the ruler of that sign?

Sun is in Scorpio and Mars is the "ruler" of Scorpio.

Step 3: When will transiting Jupiter or Saturn aspect the natal Sun position?

Saturn takes just over 29 years to make a full trip around the Zodiac. Jupiter takes just under 12 years. A quick look at the 1995 first trade horoscope in Figure 34 shows that it will be many years before Jupiter again makes a 0 degree aspect to natal Sun. In fact, Jupiter came to within reach of making a 0 degree aspect to natal Sun in early 2006. Note how share price rallied as Jupiter approached natal Sun. But, before Jupiter could complete its passage of the natal Sun location, Jupiter turned retrograde and backed up in the zodiac wheel. Note how share price then experienced a trend change and declined towards the $22 level. Once Jupiter turned Direct again in September 2006, it completed its transit past the natal Sun. The chart in Figure 35 shows the price rally that resulted as Jupiter finally passed by natal Sun. Note also that as Jupiter was completing its transit past natal Sun, restrictive Saturn was making a 90 degree aspect to natal Sun. Note how share price came under pressure as this aspect made itself known.

For the duration of 2014, Saturn will be passing by the natal Sun location. Expect some significant price volatility and perhaps some excellent short term trading opportunities.

This example illustrates the importance of Jupiter transits past the natal Sun location in the First Trade chart of a stock.

Figure 35 – CN Rail and Jupiter / Saturn transits

Step 4: When will transiting Sun or Mars make aspects to natal Sun and natal Mars locations?

During 2013 there were five transits involving natal Sun. The price chart in Figure 36 illustrates these aspects.

2013 Dates	Astrological Occurrence	Occurrence Number
January 18 to February 20	Mars and Sun pass by 90 degrees natal Sun	1
May 3 to June 5	Mars and Sun pass by 180 degrees natal Sun	2
August 7 to August 24	Sun at 90 degrees natal Sun	3
September 23 to October 18	Mars at 90 degrees to natal Sun	5
November 5 to December 2	Sun at 0 degrees natal Sun	6

Step 5: What about aspects involving the "ruler" of the Sun sign? What about aspects to natal Jupiter? What about aspects to natal Moon?

There were three dates in 2013 when these transits occurred. The price chart in Figure 36 also illustrates these aspects.

2013 Dates	Astrological Occurrence	Occurrence Number
September 5 to September 19	Sun at 90 degrees natal Jupiter, Sun 0 degrees natal Moon	4
November 5 to December 2	Mars at 0 degrees natal Moon	6
December 3 to December 17	Sun passing natal Mars and Jupiter	7

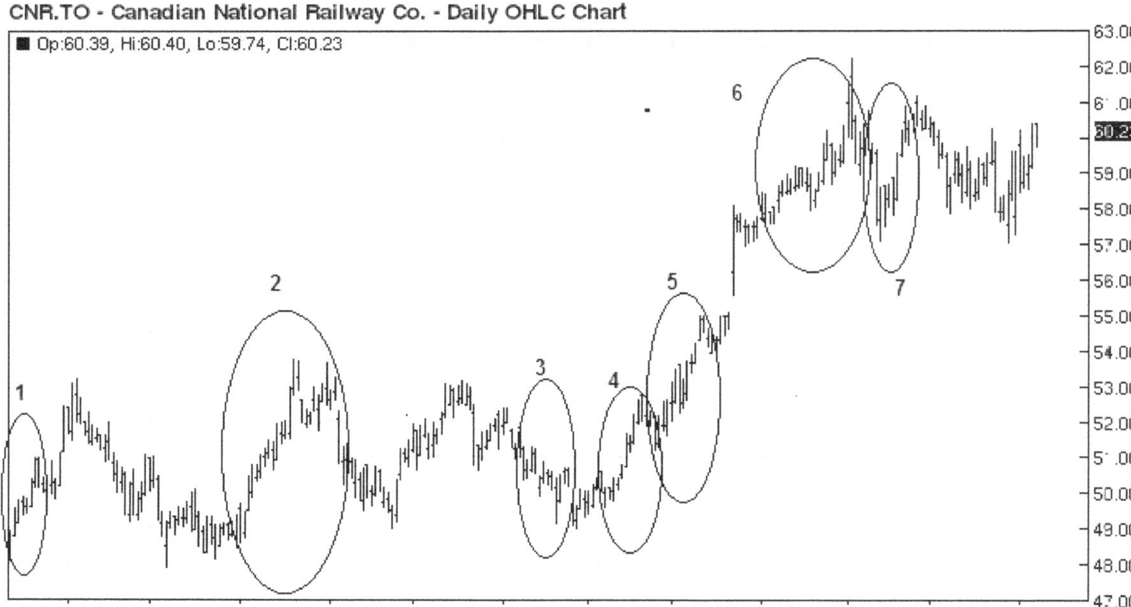

Figure 36 – CN Rail 2013 Aspects

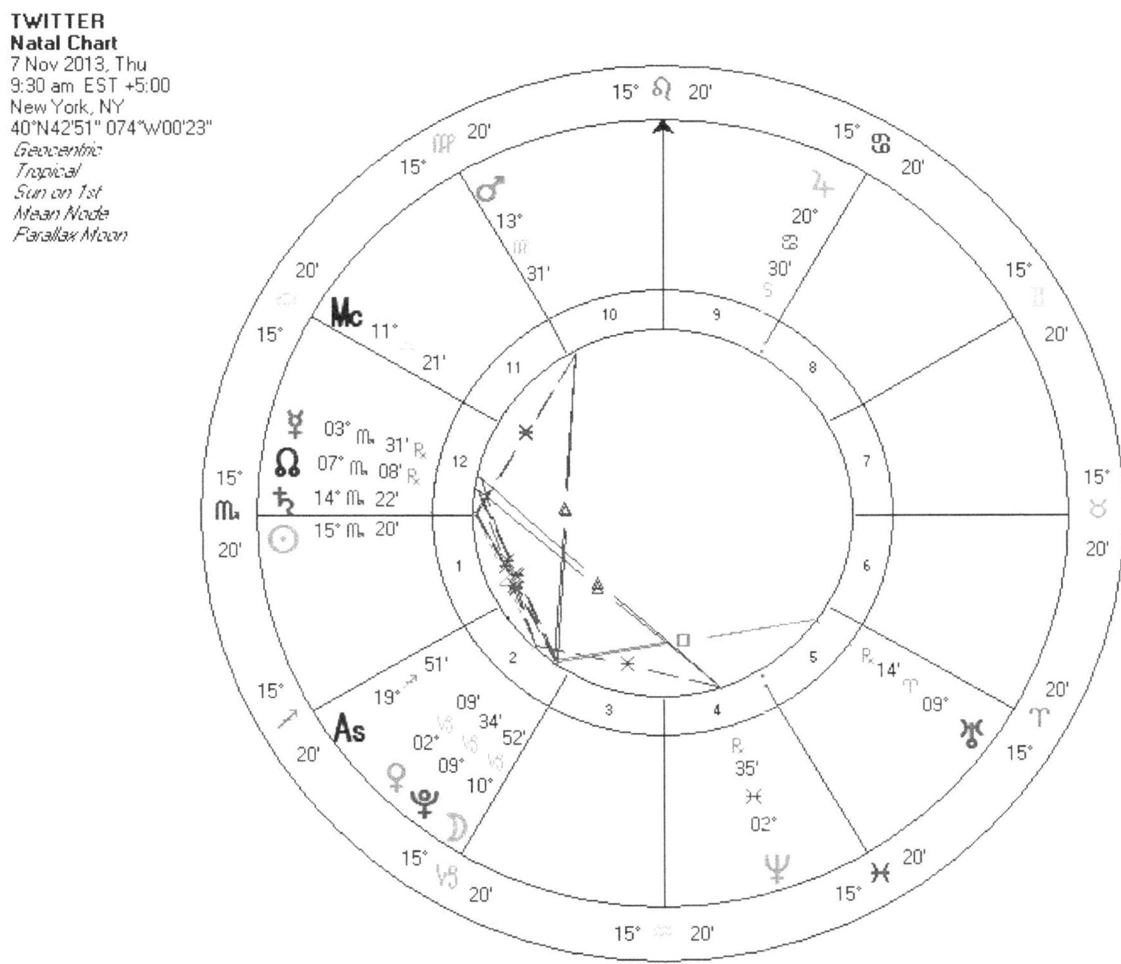

Exercise #5 - Twitter

Social messaging company Twitter started trading publicly on November 7, 2013. The planetary placements at that time are shown in this horoscope wheel.

1. Sun makes a 60 degree sextile aspect to Moon and what other planet?
2. Sun makes a conjunct aspect to what planet?
3. Moon makes a square aspect to what planet?
4. Moon makes a trine aspect to what planet?
5. When did transiting Mars pass the natal Mc position at 11Libra? What happened to price during this transit?
6. When will Mars again transit this natal MC position?

Gold Futures

Gold futures first started trading on a recognized exchange in North America on Dec 31, 1974. The horoscope in Figure 37 shows planetary positions at this time.

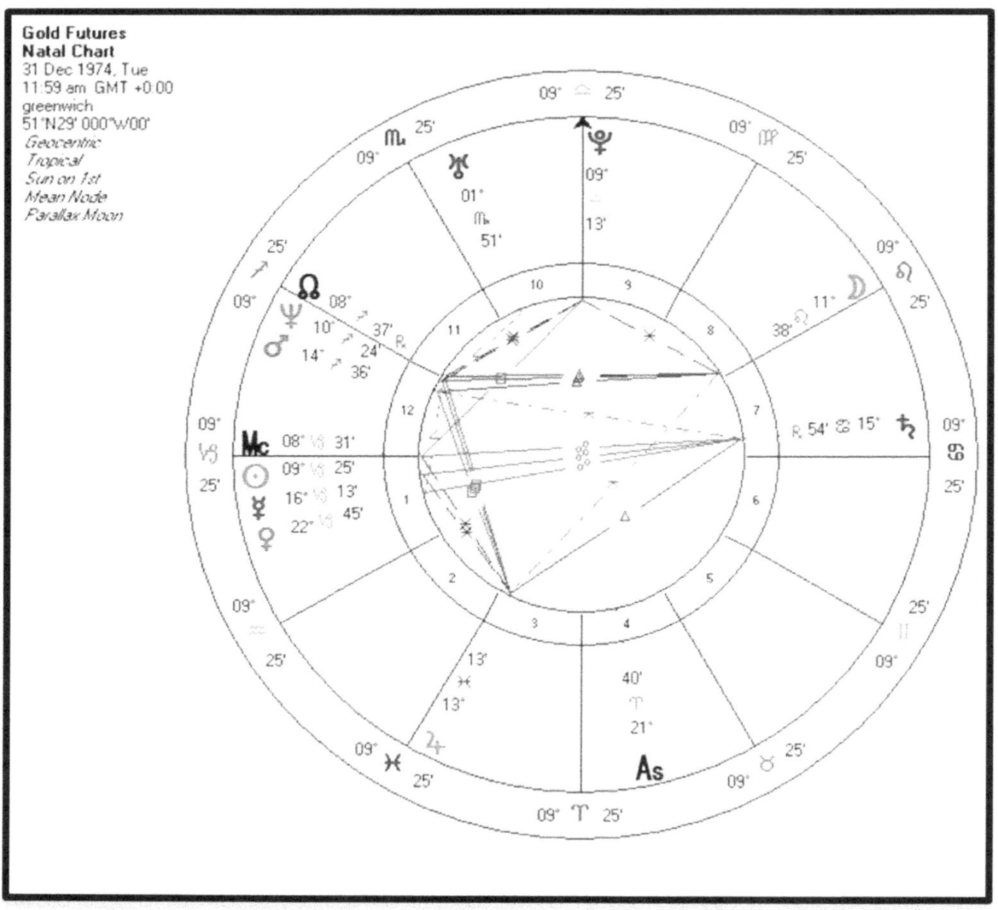

Figure 37– Gold Futures – First Trade chart

Step 1: What aspects are present to Sun, Moon and Jupiter?

Sun is 180 degrees opposite Saturn, 90 degrees square Pluto and a favorable 60 degrees to Jupiter. This aspect to Pluto is a key one indeed.

Jupiter is 120 degrees to Saturn and 90 degrees square to Mars and Neptune. Moon is 120 degrees to Mars and Neptune.

With these various complex aspects, it can be surmised that Gold futures will be volatile and not for the faint of heart.

Step 2: What sign is Sun in and what is the ruler of that sign?

Sun is in Capricorn and Saturn is the "ruler" of Capricorn. So, Sun is 180 degrees opposite to the "ruler" of its sign. This hard aspect could have interesting implications for price volatility.

Step 3: When will transiting Jupiter or Saturn aspect the natal Sun position? What about Pluto?

- In early 2008 Jupiter was at or near a 0 degree aspect to nata Sun. Jupiter spent some time Retrograde and as it finally tuned Direct again, Gold price reg stered its inflection point in late 2008 and began a march upwards.

- In early 2011, the rally in Gold price took a brief pause, but then resumed its upward push. This pause aligns to a 90 degree aspect of Jupiter to natal Sun.

-
- The 2011 high in Gold prices came as Pluto was within 4 degrees of its 90 degree hard aspect to natal Sun. Pluto also stopped being retrograde and turned direct right at the high water mark for Gold. During 2016, Pluto will complete its 90 degree hard aspect. Watch for a response in Gold prices as a result.

- The 2013 bottom in Gold prices aligns neatly to a Jupiter 180 degree aspect to natal Sun.

- From mid to late 2016, Jupiter will make a 90 degree hard aspect to natal Sun. Watch for a significant development in Gold prices then.

- During 2010 and in fact right up to late August 2011, Saturn was at or near a 90 degree aspect to natal Sun. It is interesting to note that this event had no detrimental impact on Gold price which pressed higher during this time. But – as Saturn moved out of the way – the price of Gold peaked and started to fall. This underscores an important point. Sometimes an emotional response will occur at the very beginning or very end of a transit, with little impact in between.

- During 2018, Saturn will transit past 0 degrees to natal Sun. Watch for significant developments in Gold in this timeframe.

Step 4: When will transiting Sun or Mars make aspects to natal Sun and natal Mars locations?

The weekly chart in Figure 38, which starts in late 2008 and extends for 5 years thereafter, shows those times when transiting Sun and Mars made aspects to natal Sun and natal Mars. Note the very interesting correlation to price pivot points.

Sun and Mars will make aspects to natal Sun and natal Mars on the following dates in 2014:

- March 22 to April 4 – Sun 90 degrees square natal Sun

- May 21 to July 9 – Mars 90 degrees square natal Sun and Sun 180 degrees natal Sun

- September 24 to October 15 – Sun 90 degrees natal Sun, Mars 0 degrees natal Mars

- October 27 to November 18 – Mars 0 degrees natal Sun

- November 28 to December 12 – Sun 0 degrees natal Mars

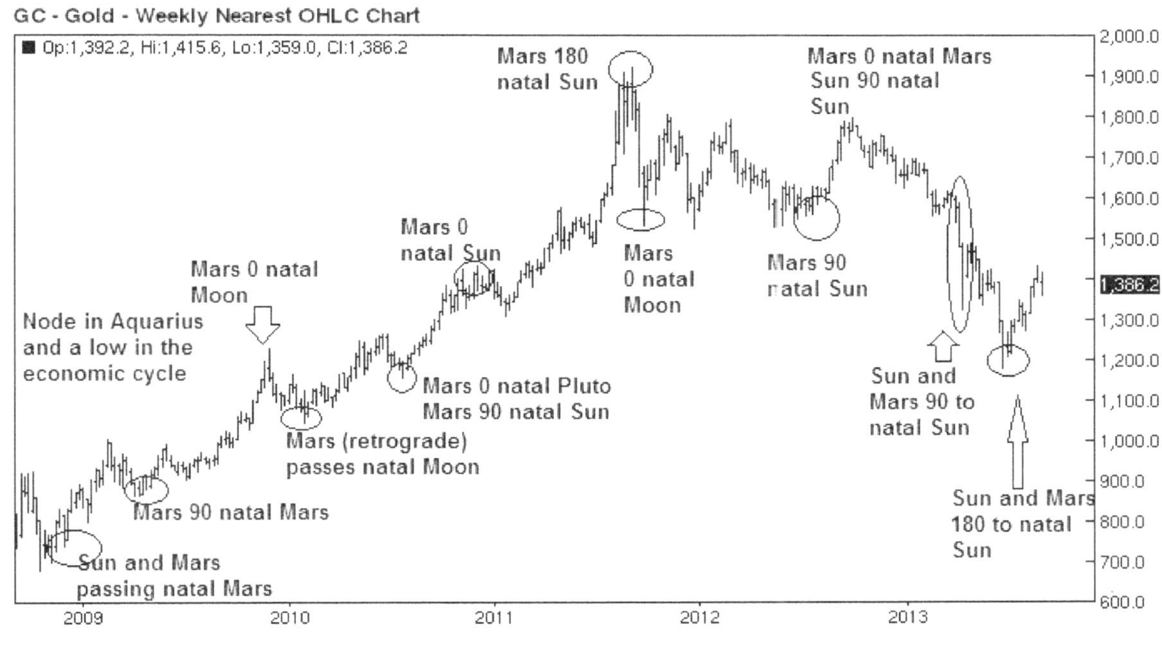

Figure 38 – Gold Futures astrological aspects

Step 5: What about aspects involving the "ruler" of the Sun sign? What about aspects to natal Jupiter and natal Moon?

Saturn is the ruler of Capricorn – the sign in which Sun appears in the first trade chart. In Step 3 above, we have already seen the effect that transiting Saturn has exerted on Gold. It is further interesting to note that the peak in Gold prices in late August 2011 came a mere two weeks after a transit of Mars past the natal Saturn location. The low in Gold price registered in mid-2013 occurred as Sun and Mars passed 180 degrees to natal Sun. Mars was also transiting past natal Saturn at this time too. By mid-June 2014 transiting Jupiter completed its transit past natal Saturn. This resulted in a significant price inflection point at the $1240 per ounce level.

The following are the 2011 dates when Gold's natal Jupiter and natal Moon were aspected.

2011 Dates	Astrological Occurrence	Occurrence Number
January 13 through January 26, 2011	Transiting Sun and Mars pass 90 degrees to natal Jupiter	1
February 27 through March 19, 2011	Transiting Sun and Mars pass natal Jupiter	2
May 26 through June 13, 2011	Sun 90 degrees natal Jupiter	3
June 24 through July 21, 2011	Mars 90 degrees natal Jupiter	4
July 27 through August 13, 2011	Transiting Sun passes natal Moon	5
September 19 through October 23, 2011	Transiting Mars passes natal Moon	6
October 27 through November 12, 2011	Transiting Sun 90 degrees natal Moon	7

Figure 39 illustrates the impact of these transits on Gold price. Note the extreme volatility associated with occurrences 5 and 6. Note how the conclusion of occurrence 7 then opened the door for a serious decline in price.

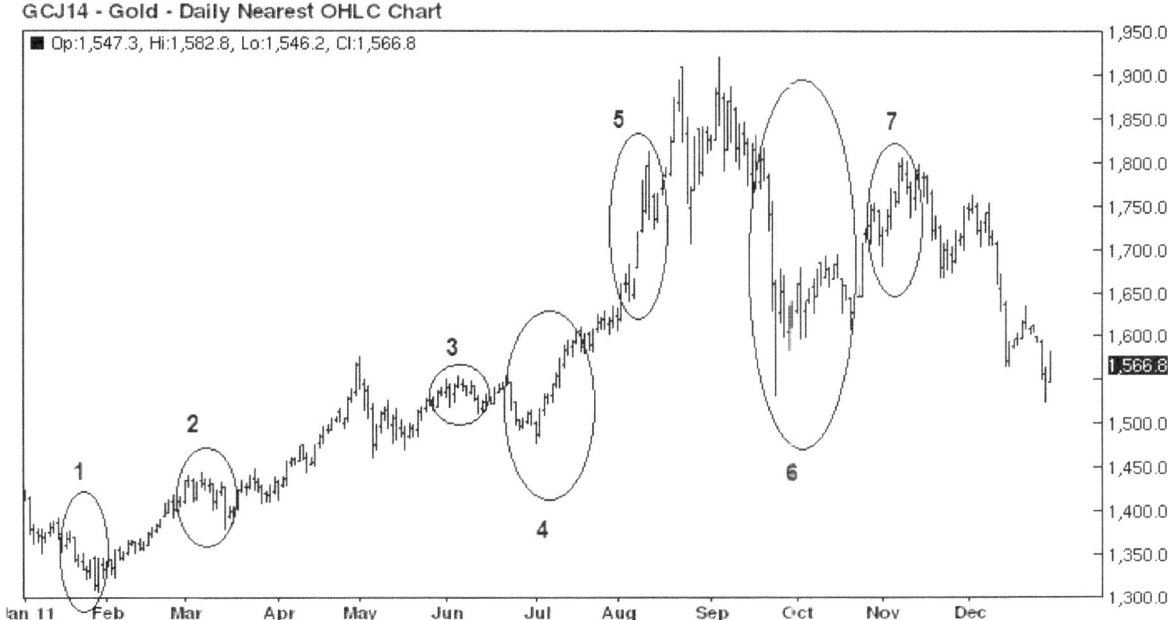

Figure 39 – 2011 Aspects to Gold natal Jupiter and natal Moon

The following are the 2012 dates when natal Gold's natal Jupiter and natal Moon were aspected.

2012 Dates	Astrological Occurrence	Occurrence Number
February 20 through March 12, 2012	Transiting Sun 0 degrees to natal Jupiter	1
April 22 through May 10, 2012	Transiting Sun 90 degrees natal Moon	2
May 24 through June 12, 2012	Sun 90 degrees natal Jupiter	3
July 23 through August 12, 2012	Transiting Sun passes natal Moon	4
August 25 through September 23, 2012	Transiting Mars 90 degrees natal Moon	5
October 7 through November 11, 2012	Transiting Mars passes 90 degrees natal Jupiter and Sun passes 90 degrees natal Moon	6
November 24 through December 14, 2012	Transiting Sun 90 degrees natal Jupiter	7

Figure 40 illustrates the impact of these transits on Gold price. Again, note the extreme volatility associated with several of these events.

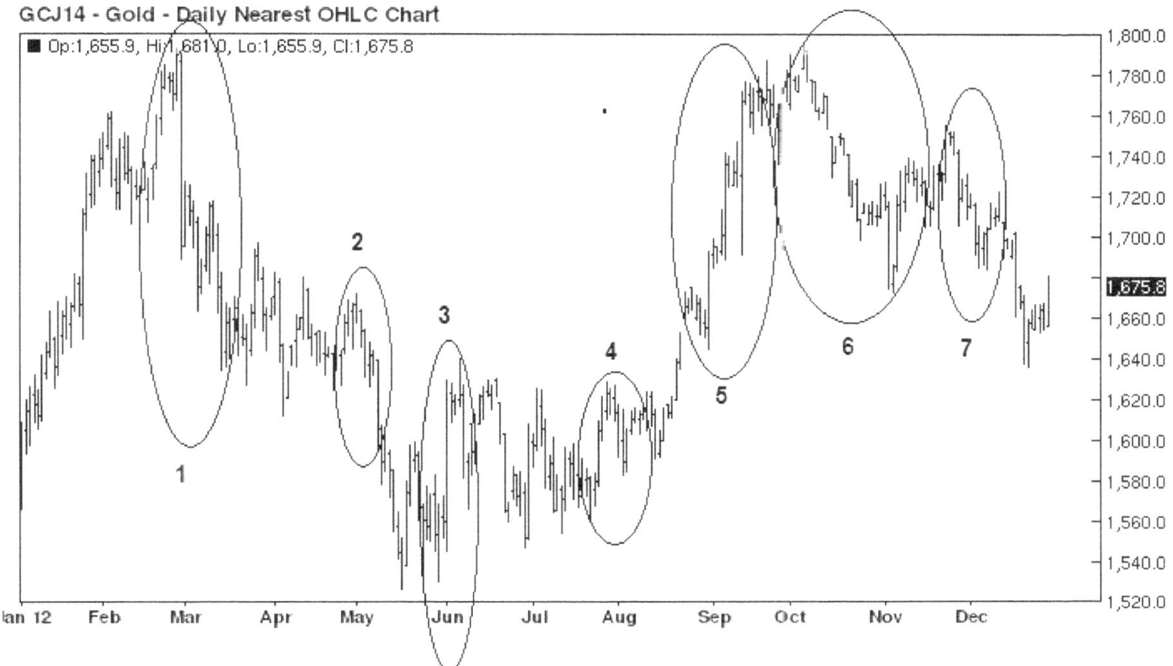

Figure 40 – 2012 Aspects to Gold natal Jupiter and natal Moon

The following are the 2013 dates when Gold's natal Jupiter and natal Moon were aspected.

2013 Dates	Astrological Occurrence	Occurrence Number
February 6 through March 12, 2013	Transiting Sun and Mars 0 degrees to natal Jupiter	1
April 22 through May 17, 2013	Transiting Sun and Mars 90 degrees natal Moon	2
May 25 through June 30, 2013	Transiting Sun and Mars 90 degrees natal Jupiter	3
July 25 through August 13, 2013	Transiting Sun 0 degrees natal Moon	4
August 31 through September 29, 2013	Transiting Mars 0 degrees natal Moon	5
October 26 through November 12, 2013	Transiting Sun 90 degrees natal Moon	6
November 30 through December 13, 2013	Transiting Sun 90 degrees natal Jupiter	7

Figure 41 illustrates the impact of these transits on Gold price. Again, note the extreme volatility associated with several of these events.

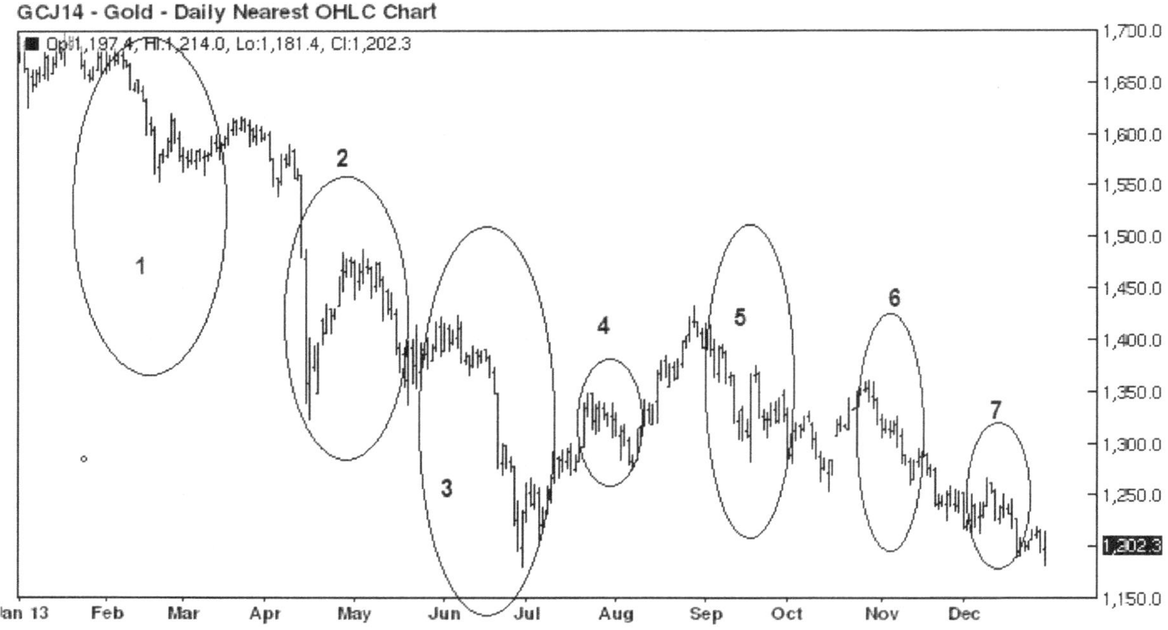

Figure 41 - 2013 Aspects to Gold natal Jupiter and natal Moon

This Gold futures example reinforces once again that when applying astrology and the McWhirter technique, it often can help to examine Fibonacci retracement levels on price charts. A detailed explanation of Fibonacci retracements can be found in my book *The Lost Science*.

In the case of Gold, as we have seen in Figure 38, price made a significant inflection point low in late 2008 at $700. Gold then reached a peak in price at $1920 in the Autumn of 2011. The Fibonacci retracements levels that every trader and investor should examine include 0.114, 0.300, 0.382, 0.486, 0.618 and 0.786. The general formula for determining these levels is given by $1/(\text{sq.root (phi)}^n)$, where phi is 1.618 (the Golden Mean) and n=1,2,3,4,5,6,7,8,9.

The weekly chart in Figure 42 shows where these various retracement ratios occur. When applying the McWhirter method, watch carefully for price action to touch a Fibonacci retracement level as an astrological event occurs. This chart shows that in late 2013 Gold price re-tested the 0.618 retracement level. Curiously enough, at that time Mars was also making its 90 degree aspect to natal Sun.

Figure 42 – Gold and Fibonacci retracements

Exercise #6 – The Node

McWhirter was wary of aspects between the North Node and Saturn and between the North Node and Uranus. Uranus in Gemini was also said to be problematic for the economy.

Using either your Ephemeris Tables or your software program, look forward to see when the following events occur :

1. North Node 180 degrees to Uranus
2. Saturn 90 degrees square to North Node
3. Saturn 180 degrees to North Node
4. North Node 0 degrees to Uranus
5. Uranus in Gemini
6. When was the last time Uranus was in Gemini?

Soybean Futures

Soybean futures first started trading on a recognized exchange in North America on October 5, 1936. The horoscope in Figure 43 shows planetary positions at this time.

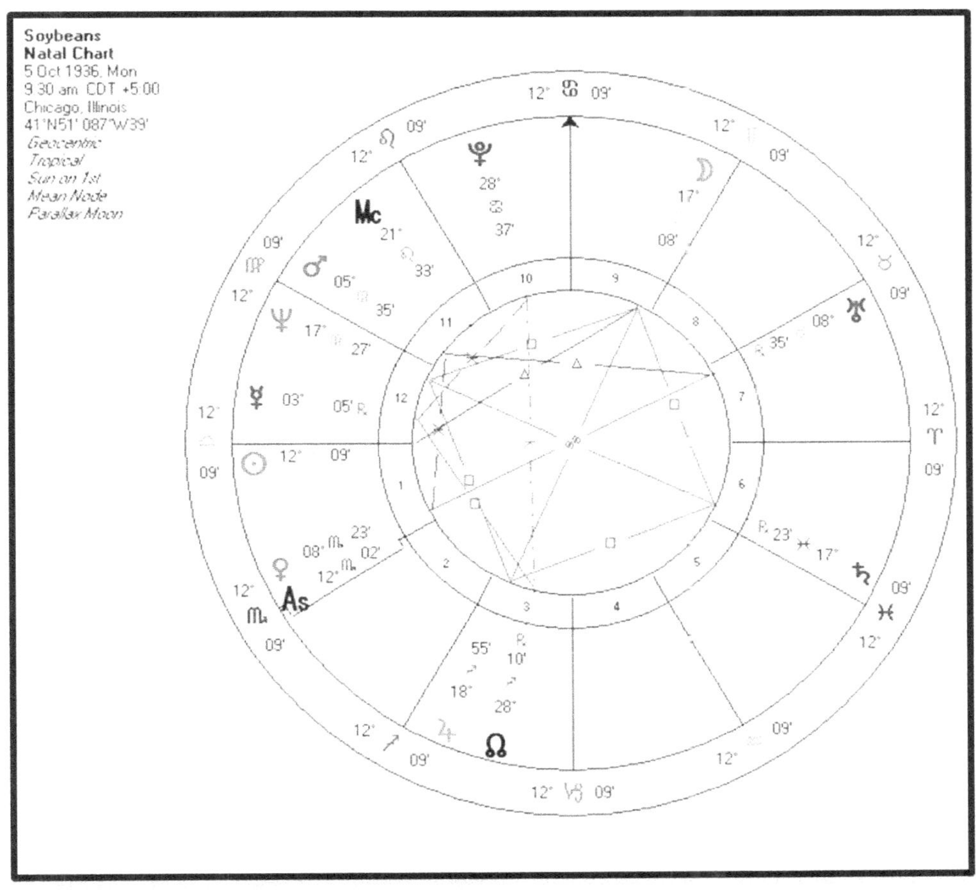

Figure 43 - Soybean Futures First Trade chart

Step 1: What aspects are present to Sun, Moon and Jupiter?

Sun is 120 degrees to Moon. Moon in turn is 90 degrees square Saturn, 90 degrees square Neptune and 180 degrees opposite Jupiter. Jupiter is 90 degrees square Saturn and Neptune. Collectively, these aspects form a square pattern called a Grand Cross. Such patterns are infrequent and must be respected for hints they may offer.

Step 2: What sign is Sun in and what is the ruler of that sign?

Sun is in Libra and Venus is the "ruler" of Libra.

Step 3: When will transiting Jupiter or Saturn aspect the natal Sun position?

- Transiting Saturn passed the natal Sun location between August 2010 and early February 2011. Saturn then turned Retrograde and backed up in the zodiac wheel. From mid-June 2011 to early November 2011, Saturn completed its passage of the natal Sun location. The weekly nearest price chart in Figure 44 illustrates the significant moves associated with these Saturn events. Saturn will make a 90 degree aspect to natal Sun in 2018, so there is no need to worry about Saturn until then.

- In early 2011, Jupiter made a 180 degree aspect to natal Sun. Price action of Soybeans at the time confined to a sideways channel and this Jupiter aspect exerted little effect on the situation. Price was finally shaken out of its sideways channel in late August when Mars made a 90 degree hard aspect to natal Sun. In mid to late Summer 2012, Jupiter was making a 120 degree aspect to natal Sun. This event aligned to the price peak that was being recorded in the Bean market as a result of what the financial media deemed to be a severe drought. Figure 45 illustrates further.

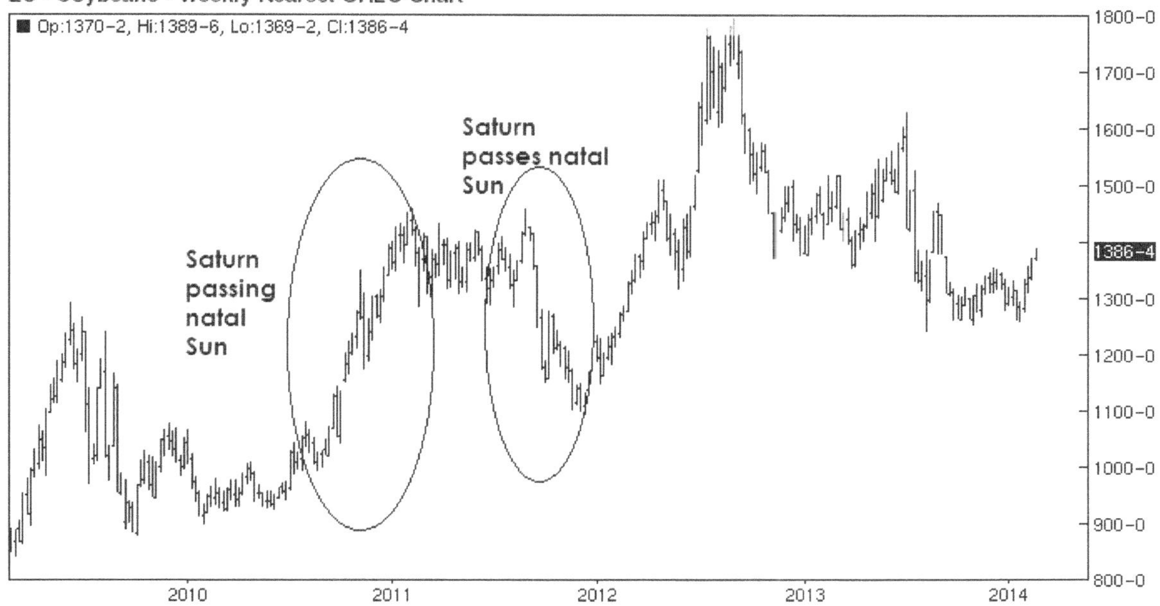

Figure 44 - Saturn and Soybeans

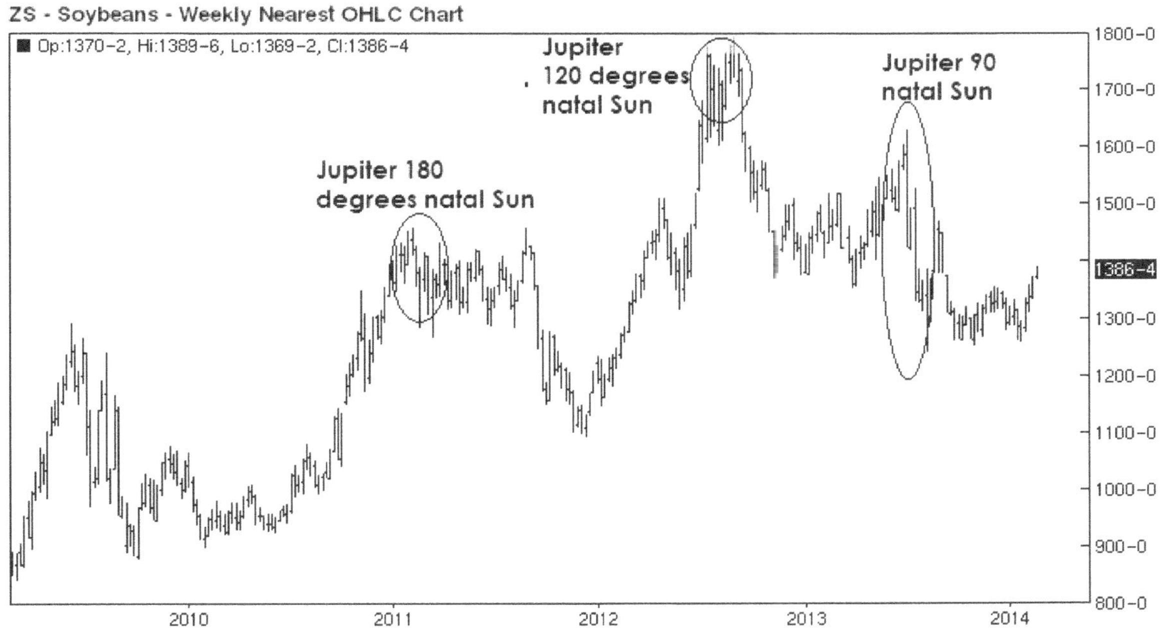

Figure 45 - Jupiter and Soybeans

Step 4: When will transiting Sun or Mars make aspects to natal Sun and natal Mars locations?

The weekly chart in Figure 46 shows those times when transiting Mars made aspects to natal Sun and natal Mars.

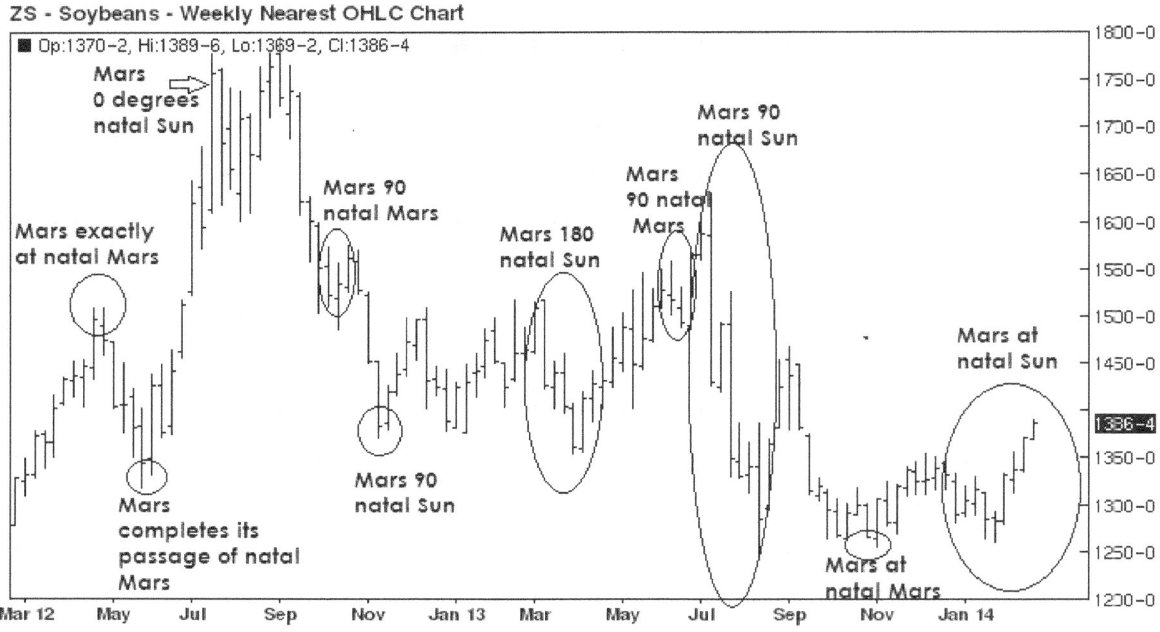

Figure 46 - Mars and Soybeans

Mars will turn Retrograde on March 1, 2014. By the third week of May, Mars will be ready to resume its Direct motion. As it does, it will transit past natal Sun by early July. During the first several weeks of November 2014, Mars will complete a 90 degree aspect to natal Sun. From late June to mid-July, transiting Sun will make a 90 degree aspect to natal Sun. From late September to early October, a transit past natal Sun will occur. From late December to early January 2015, a 90 degree aspect will occur.

Step 5: What about aspects involving the "ruler" of the Sun sign? What about aspects to natal Jupiter and natal Moon?

Figure 47 illustrates several incidents where transiting Sun and/or Mars made aspects to the natal Venus location.

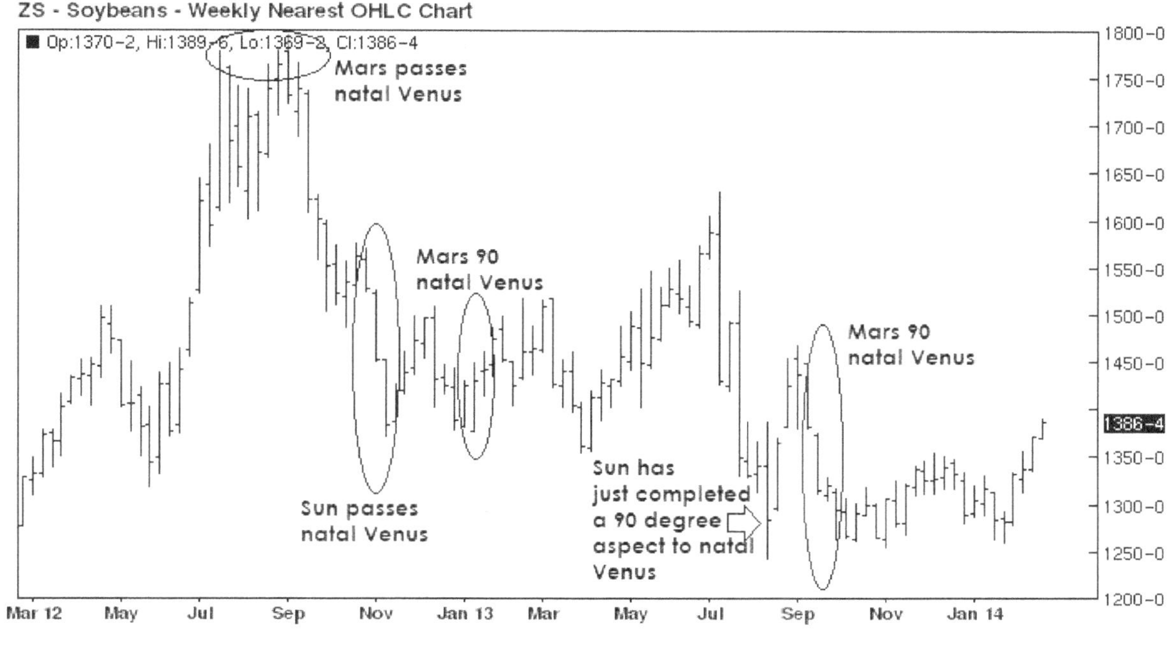

Figure 47 – Venus and Soybeans

In this Soybeans example we have already seen how astrological aspects align to the price highs in 2012. Here we see yet another alignment in the form of transiting Mars passing the natal Venus location. The sell-off that occurred after the 2012 price peak was arrested in November 2012 as Sun passed natal Venus. A price low in August 2013 occurred just as Sun wrapped up a 90 degree aspect to natal Venus. A sharp sell-off in September 2013 took place as Mars made a 90 degree aspect to natal Venus.

During the first half of March, 2014 transiting Sun will make a 90 degree aspect to the natal Moon location and a 90 degree aspect to the natal Jupiter location.

During the first half of June, 2014 transiting Sun will pass by the natal Moon location and make a 180 degree aspect to the natal Jupiter location.

During the first half of September, 2014 transiting Sun will make a 90 degree aspect to the natal Moon location and a 90 degree aspect to natal Jupiter.

During the first half of December, 2014 transiting Sun will make a 180 degree aspect to the natal Moon location and a 0 degree aspect to natal Jupiter.

In Figure 47, note that Soybean prices hit a high at just over $16 per bushel in July 2013 and then started to decline. At this time of preparing this manuscript for publication, the price weakness continues. The culprit behind this weakness is Uranus and its 180 degree aspect to natal Sun. By the first quarter of 2015, this transit will be complete and a return to more robust Soybean prices should follow.

Wheat and Corn Futures

Wheat, Corn and Oats futures started trading in Chicago on January 2 back in 1877.

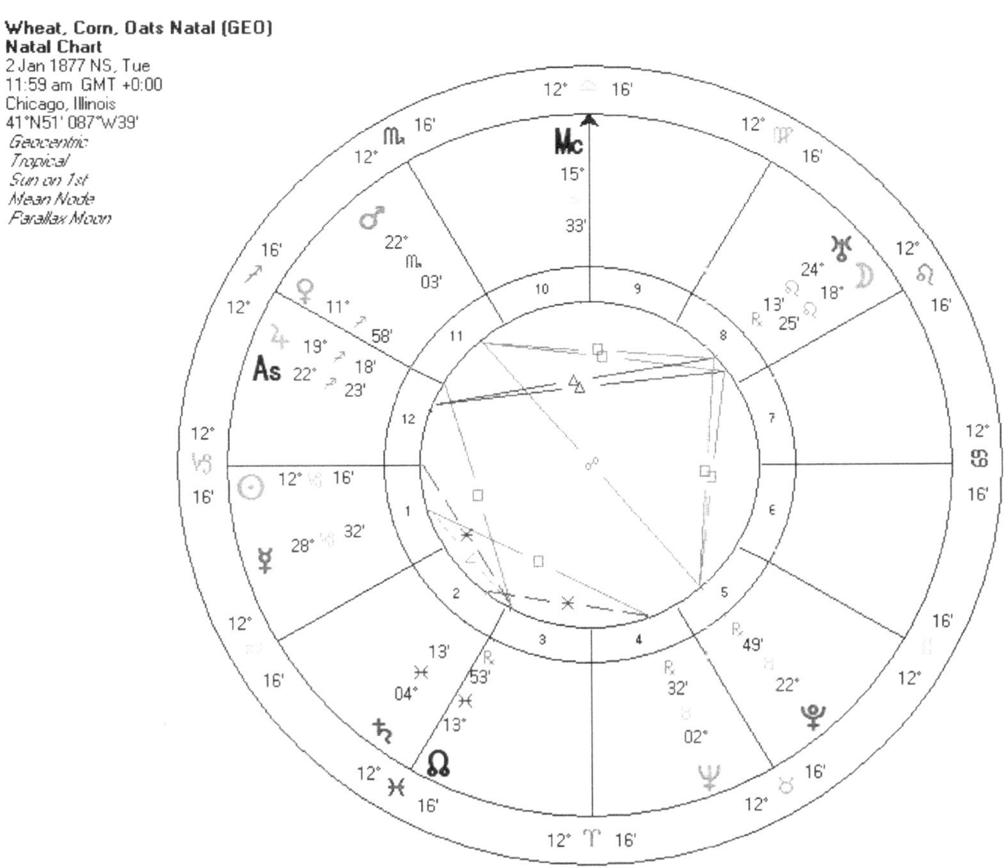

Figure 48 Wheat, Corn, Oats natal horoscope

Step 1: What aspects are present to Sun, Moon and Jupiter?

Sun makes no aspects with other planets. Moon is just within orb of being 90 degrees to Mars. Moon is also within orb of being 0 degrees conjunct to Uranus. Jupiter makes no aspects to other planets.

Step 2: What sign is Sun in and what is the ruler of that sign?

Sun is in Capricorn and Saturn is the "ruler" of Capricorn.

Step 3: When will transiting Jupiter or Saturn aspect the natal Sun position?

- Transiting Saturn last passed the natal Sun location in late 1989-early 1990. It will again transit past natal Sun in 2018.

- In early 1996, Jupiter made a 180 degree aspect to natal Sun. Price action of Corn at the time powered higher, rising from $3.60 to $5.00 per bushel – a big move for markets back then. Wheat turned in a similar performance, rising from $3.50 to $4.50 per bushel. In early 2008, as Jupiter again passed natal Sun, Wheat prices fell from $6.40 to $5.00 per bushel. Corn fell from $4.30 to $3.40 a bushel with this same Jupiter transit.

Step 4: When will transiting Sun or Mars make aspects to natal Sun and natal Mars locations?

The weekly chart in Figure 49 illustrates those times when transiting Sun made hard aspects (0,90,180 degrees) to natal Sun and natal Mars.

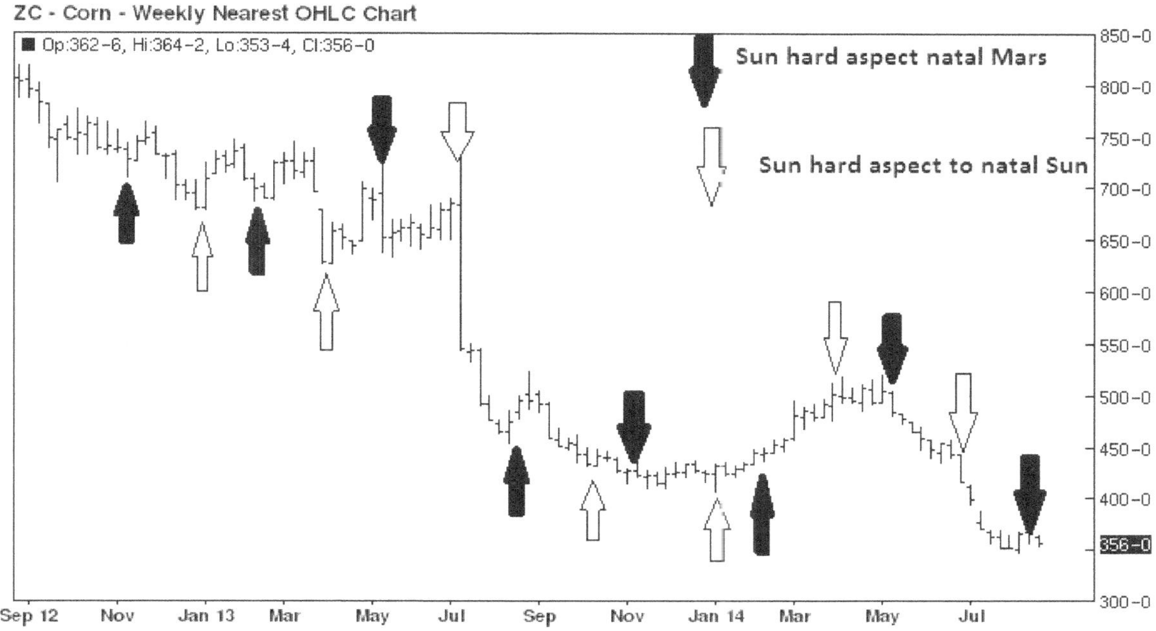

Figure 49 Corn and Sun making hard aspects to natal Sun and natal Mars

This example of Wheat and Corn has been included to further illustrate the very potent aspect of Uranus. The planet Uranus takes some 82 years to fully make an orbit around the twelve signs of the zodiac. Periods in time when slow-moving Uranus makes hard aspects to natal Sun must be taken seriously. In the September 2012, Uranus came to within 7 degrees of the natal Sun location of Wheat and Corn. Uranus then turned Retrograde and retreated somewhat. In December 2012, Uranus again began to advance on the 90 degree aspect to natal sun. As Figure 49 illustrates, this timeframe aligns to the start of a serious price drop on Corn futures. Although not illustrated here, a similar response is clearly evident on a Wheat futures chart. As this manuscript goes to publication, North American farmers are very nervous and many agricultural type equities have fallen in value. The good news is that by the first quarter of 2015, Uranus will have moved past the 90 degree aspect and a return to higher grain prices should be underway.

Euro Currency

The Euro became the official currency of the European Union on January 1, 2002. However, prior to that date, there was some circulation of physical bank notes in Europe starting on January 1, 1999. Taking this date as being the First Trade date for the currency, the following horoscope illustrates planetary positions at that time.

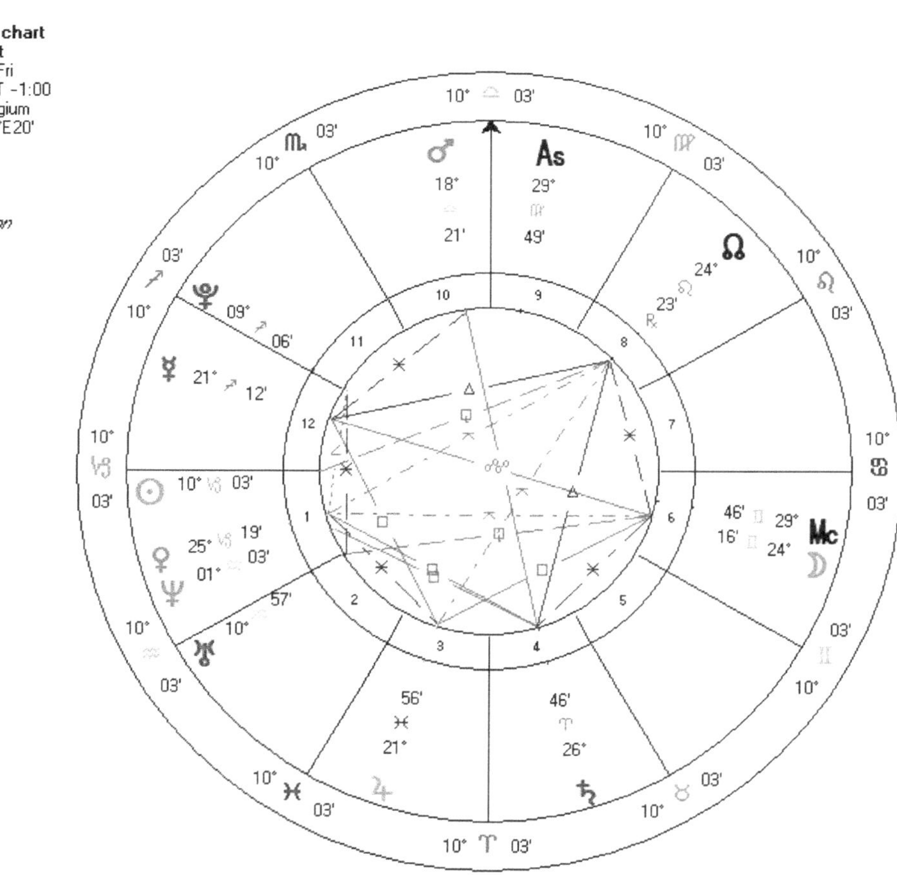

Figure 50 Euro Currency First Trade chart

Step 1: What aspects are present to Sun, Moon and Jupiter?

In this chart there are no aspects to the Sun. Jupiter is 90 degrees square to Moon and also to Mercury.

Step 2: What sign is Sun in and what is the ruler of that sign?

Sun is in Capricorn and Saturn is the "ruler" of Capricorn.

Step 3: When will transiting Jupiter or Saturn aspect the natal Sun position?

Transiting Jupiter transited past the natal Sun location between February and March of 2008. During this transit, the value of the Euro rose smartly from 1.45 ($US per Euro) to the 1.60 level. But, this rally would turn out to be one of false hope. After hitting the $1.60 level, the Euro sufferted a massive loss of value and the $1.60 level has not since been re-visited.

In early 2019, Saturn will make its transit past the natal Sun location. This could herald some big changes for the Euro, if it is still intact then. There are many naysayers who are calling for significant change to the Euro right now and there are nations in the E.U. right now who are openly talking about leaving the common currency. This is no doubt the influence of Pluto which is currently transiting past the natal Sun location. Pluto will complete its transit during 2015. Look for the Euro to be in the news a fair bit in 2015.

Step 4: When will transiting Sun or Mars make aspects to natal Sun and natal Mars locations?

The weekly chart in Figure 51 illustrates some recent Sun and Mars transits.

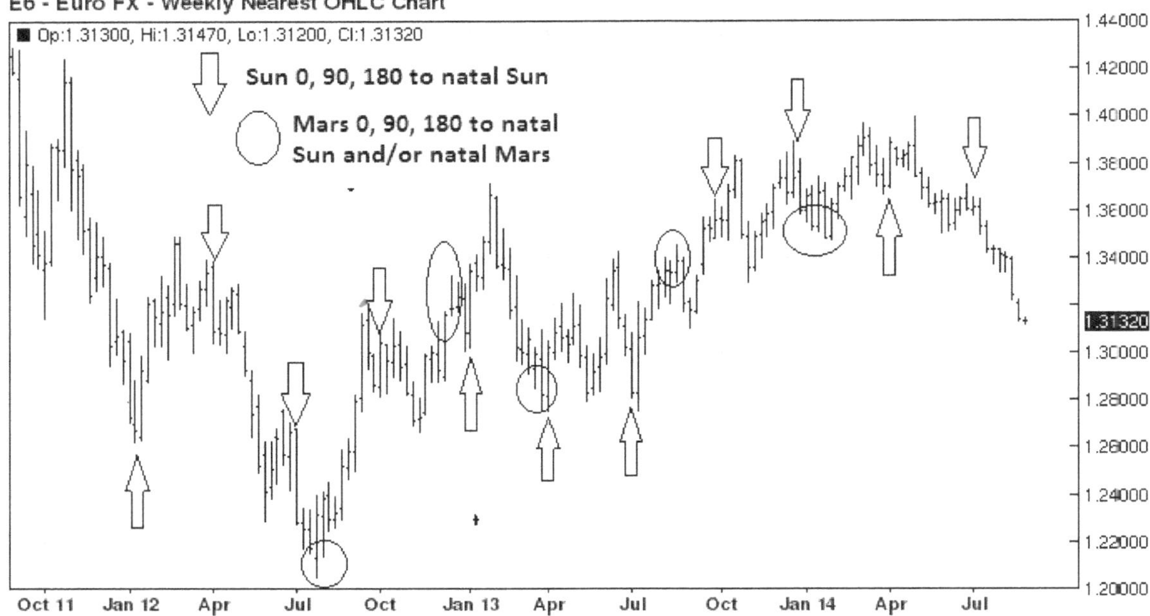

Figure 51 – Transiting Sun and Mars aspects

Step 5: What about aspects involving the "ruler" of the Sun sign? What about aspects to natal Jupiter and natal Moon?

Figure 52 illustrates aspects between transiting Sun and natal Moon as well as natal Jupiter. Although not illustrated in Figure 52, there can be seen to exist a short term reaction in price in mid-January, Mid-April, mid-July and mid-October as Sun makes 0, 90 and 180 degree aspects to natal Saturn.

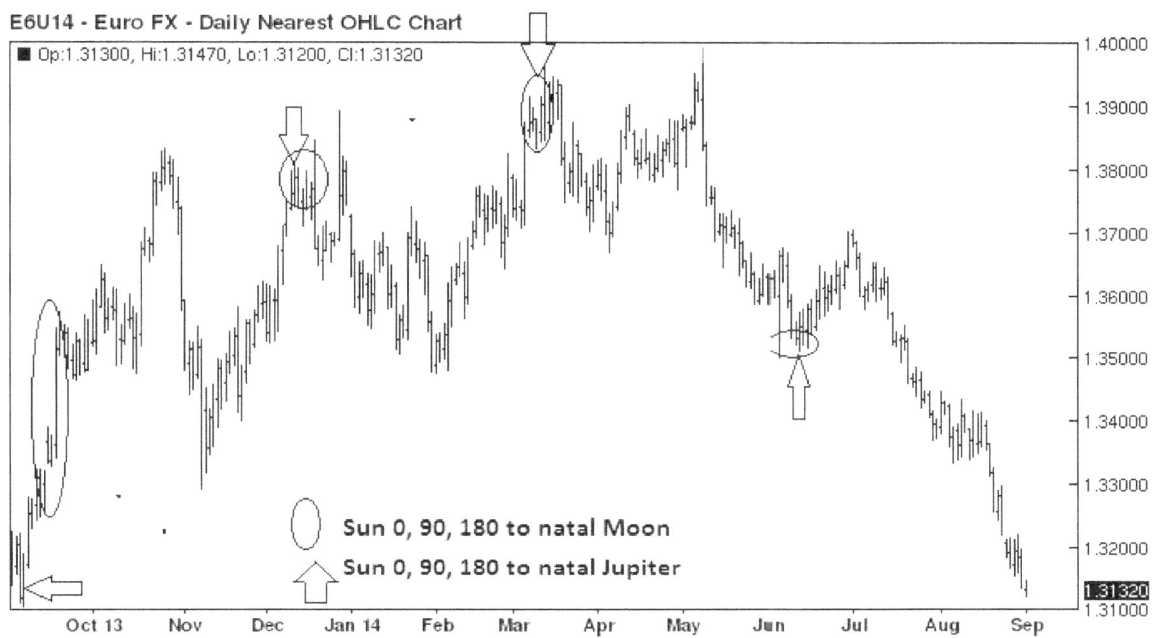

Figure 52 Aspects to natal Moon and Jupiter

13. CONCLUDING REMARKS FROM THE AUTHOR

The publication has covered a lot of material in a short time. You are now in possession of skills that few other traders and investors have. To keep those skills sharp, I recommend practice, practice, practice. Look at charts of commodity futures. Look at charts of individual stocks. Look at the corresponding First Trade horoscopes. Identify the various astrological events that have best aligned to price trend changes. The more of this practice you undertake, the better you will become at applying the McWhirter methodology.

As you apply the McWhirter methodology to your trading and investing, be sure to always bear in mind that astrological aspects can take time to unfold. Observing price action closely for evidence of short term trend change (and thus your trade entry point) is important as the astrological aspect occurs. Use short term technical chart indicators and charting techniques to help you identify the change of trend. Also, be sure to keep a close tab on Fibonacci retracements and extensions, especially those that are occurring as an astrological occurrence is due to manifest itself. And above all else, always be mindful of your risk tolerance.

I welcome questions from you once you have worked your way through this manuscript. As always, I can be reached at astrologicaltrader@gmail.com

14. DE-BRIEF

Exercise #1

1. Where is the Asc located in this horoscope of the New York Stock Exchange?

The Asc is located at 14 degrees in the sign of Cancer.

2. Where is the MC located in this horoscope?

The MC is located at 24 degrees in the sign of Pisces.

3. Which signs comprise the 10th House?

Aries and Pisces are the two signs that comprise the 10th House.

<u>Exercise #2</u>

1. What is the sign and degree position of Jupiter?

Jupiter is in the sign of Aries at 18 degrees.

2. Does the Sun make an aspect angle to Jupiter?

Sun is separated from Sun by 5 degrees and this is a conjunction aspect.

3. What is the aspect relation between Jupiter and Saturn?

Jupiter and Saturn are separated by 175 degrees and this is an opposition aspect.

4. What is the sign and degree position of Moon?

Moon is in the sign of Leo at 17 degrees.

<u>Exercise #3</u>

1.   What sign is Sun located in?

Sun is in the sign of Capricorn.

2.   What is the ruler of this sign?

Saturn rules Capricorn

3.   To which planet does Sun make a 180 degree aspect?

Sun is 180 degrees to Pluto

4.   To which planets does Jupiter make aspects to? Describe these aspects.

Jupiter makes 180 degree aspects to Neptune and Mars

5.   To what planet does Moon make an aspect to? Describe this aspect.

Moon makes a 120 degree aspect to Uranus

6.   When will Saturn again transit past natal Sun?

Saturn will transit past natal Sun during 2017-2018.

Exercise #4

1. In what sign does the Mid-Heaven (MC) appear?

In the sign of Aries

2. What is the ruler of that sign?

Mars rules Aries

3. What celestial bodies are conjunct to the MC?

Sun is 2 degrees from the MC and Mercury is 6 degrees away. These separations meet the criteria as dictated by McWhirter for a conjunction type aspect.

4. A rectangular shape can be seen in this horoscope wheel. Which celestial bodies make up this rectangular shape?

Mars at 25 degrees of Aries, Neptune at 29 degrees Sagittarius, Pluto at 28 Libra and North Node at 29 Gemini are the 4 points that constitute the rectangle.

It could also be said that Mars at 25 degrees of Aries, Neptune at 29 degrees Sagittarius, Saturn at 2 degrees Scorpio, and North Node at 29 Gemini are the 4 points that constitute the rectangle.

It could also be said that Mars at 25 degrees of Aries, Neptune at 29 degrees Sagittarius, Moon at 1 degree Scorpio, and North Node at 29 Gemini are the 4 points that constitute the rectangle.

Exercise #5

1. Sun makes a 60 degree sextile aspect to Moon and what other planet?

Mars is the other planet that Sun makes a sextile aspect to.

2. Sun makes a conjunct aspect to what planet?

Saturn

3. Moon makes a square aspect to what planet?

Uranus

4. Moon makes a trine aspect to what planet?

Mars

5. When did transiting Mars pass the natal MC position at 11Libra? What happened to price during this transit?

From Dec 12th, 2013 to January 19th, 2014 Mars was completing this transit. During this transit share price rose from ~$58 to just shy of $75 and then fell back down to ~$58 as Mars completed its transit.

6. When will Mars again transit this natal MC position?

In about December 2015.

Exercise #6

1. North Node 180 degrees to Uranus
From June 2014 to April 2015

2. Saturn 90 degrees square to North Node
February 2016 to November 2016

3. Saturn 180 degrees to North Node
February 2019 to December 2019

4. North Node 0 degrees to Uranus
April 2022 to March 2023

5. Uranus in Gemini

July 2025 through October 2025 after which Uranus will appear Retrograde in the sign of Taurus

Uranus will turn Direct again and will be in Gemini from May 2026 through August 2032

6. When was the last time Uranus was in Gemini?

Uranus was last in Gemini from August 1941 through October 1941 and then from May 1942 through October 1948. Collectively these years can best be described as the World War 2 years.

APPENDIX

McWhirter New Moon Analysis Worksheet

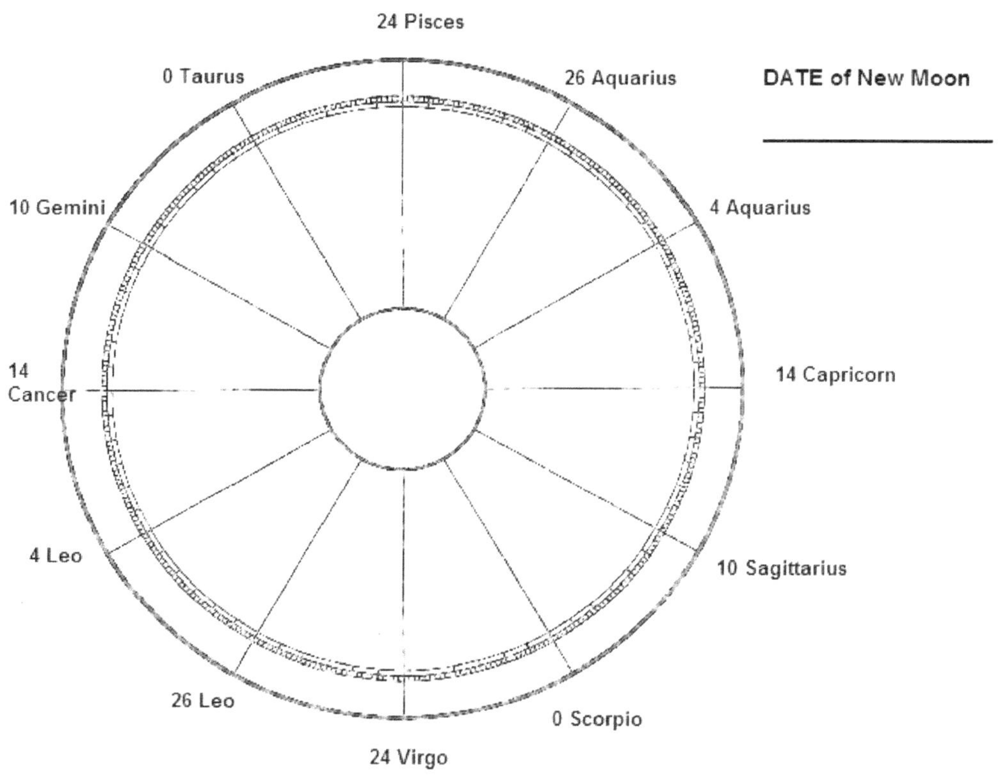

First Trade Date

Stock Ticker Symbol

SUN

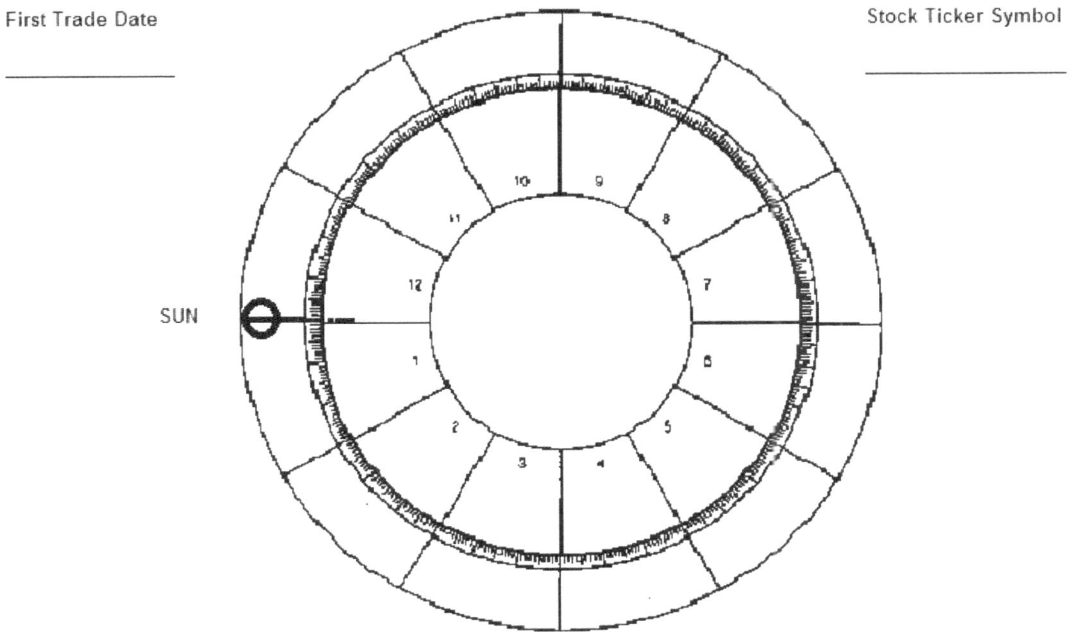

McWhirter Analysis of Individual Stocks

ABOUT THE AUTHOR

Malcolm Bucholtz, B.Sc, MBA is a graduate of Queen's University Faculty of Engineering in Canada and Heriot Watt University in Scotland where he received an MBA degree. After working in Canadian industry for far too many years, Malcolm followed his passion for the financial markets by becoming an Investment Advisor/Commodity Trading Advisor with an independent brokerage firm in western Canada. Today, he resides in western Canada where he trades the financial markets using technical chart analysis, esoteric mathematics and the astrological principles outlined in this book.

Malcolm is the author of four previous books. His first book, *The Bull, the Bear and the Planets*, offers the reader an introduction to Financial Astrology and makes the case that there are esoteric and astrological phenomena that influence the financial markets. His second book, *The Lost Science*, takes the reader on a deeper journey into planetary events and unique mathematical phenomena that influence financial markets. His third and fourth books, *The 2014 Financial Astrology Almanac* and *The 2015 Financial Astrology Almanac* use the McWhirter method to identify those critical dates in 2014 and 2015 respectively when selected commodity futures contracts and also the New York Stock Exchange are likely to experience trend changes.

This book, *Stock Market Forecasting – The McWhirter Method De-Mystified* was initially crafted in early 2014 without an ISBN number and sold from my website under the title *De-Mystifying the McWhirter Theory of Stock Market Forecasting – A Study Guide*. The demand for this material has led to the decision to assign a proper ISBN number to it and to retail it through proper channels.

Malcolm maintains both a website (www.investingsuccess.ca) and a blog (www.astrologicaltrading.wordpress.com) where he provides traders and investors with astrological insights into the financial markets. He also offers a monthly **Astrology E-Alert** service where subscribers receive a weekly preview of pending astrological events that stand to influence markets.